THE DIARY OF PETER POWNALL

A BRAMHALL FARMER   1765-1858

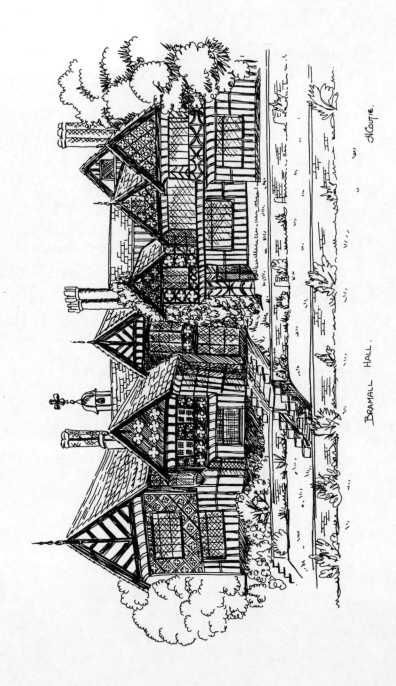

BRAMALL HALL.

JJ Coutie.

THE DIARY OF PETER POWNALL

A BRAMHALL FARMER 1765-1858

An Introduction to Local History

Edited and illustrated by
Heather Coutie

OLD VICARAGE PUBLICATIONS

Congleton

The Diary of Peter Pownall: A Bramhall Farmer 1765-1858
Copyright (Editorial Matter & Illustrations) 1989 Heather Coutie

Published for

Stockport Historical Society

by

Old Vicarage Publications
Reades Lane, Dane in Shaw,
Congleton, Cheshire, CW12 3LL

Printed by
Billings & Sons Limited
Hylton Road
Worcester, WR2 5JU

British Library Cataloguing in Publication Data
Pownall, Peter, 1765-1858
  The diary of Peter Pownall : a Bramhall farmer, 1765-1858 :
  an introduction to local history.
  1. England. Local history. Historical sources
  I. Title   II. Coutie, Heather
  942

  ISBN 0-947818-59-6

THE DIARY OF PETER POWNALL : A BRAMHALL FARMER 1765-1858.

INTRODUCTION

It all started several years ago when a photocopy of a diary written by a Bramhall farmer at the end of the eighteenth century was given to me and I showed it to my then WEA local history class. They expressed interest in transcribing it and, once done, it occurred to me that it would make a good basis for a project in practical local history. After the class closed some members remained interested and we formed a group under the auspices of the Stockport Historical Society to continue the work. It was realised that many of the books used for reference by beginners in local history, school children for projects and such like, assumed a standard of knowledge not always possessed. I decided to use the work as a practical guide for those who want to know more about the lives of people in the past. The diary ilustrates details of eighteenth century Cheshire, its agriculture, social customs, and most particularly the manor and people of a typical Cheshire village, Bramhall.

I hope that the book will appeal to the lover of family history who wants to discover more about the lives of his ancestors, whether from this area or further afield. Also that it will help the beginner researching local history, whether finding out about his own house or the village or town in which he lives; for although based on Bramhall, it explains many of the words and phrases used in a wider area. It is also written for schoolchildren researching history projects for their studies, which may introduce them to obscure or archaic expressions that are not easily understood. Finally the book is for all those who want to know more of the history of Bramhall and this part of Cheshire, who will find plenty to interest them.

The book is in four parts; the transcribed diary, the glossary which is based on the diary but contains a wide range of information on the interpretation of records, the appendix which contains examples of the records, and finally the bibliography and index.

The Diary

The diary, which is divided into several parts, was started in October 1782 by Peter Pownall, who was only seventeen at the time. Sadly, like so many diarists, he stopped his daily entries seven years later in March 1789 but later re-used it for his farm accounts. These contain records of sales from August 1794 to June 1805; receipts and payments for the period November 1806 to November 1808; and, between July 1796 and August 1812, he used the book to note the hours worked by his casual, harvest labourers. A transcription of the diary only has been printed, although transcripts of the whole have been given to Stockport Library Study Room and the University of Reading for the use of readers.

In the printing the original format of the pages has been retained and they are numbered as such but to save space they have been printed together. The following conventions have been used in the transcription: the original spelling, use of capitals and punctuation have been retained; contracted words have been extended within []; words which are not clear are prefixed [?] and illegible words are noted thus [illegible]. The capitals H and K are identical in the original so the context has decided their use. (For example see Hilled in the Glossary)

The Glossary

Instead of extensive footnotes it was decided to provide a glossary to assist the reader who wanted to understand many of the more obscure references in the diary, and the local history behind it. Words in the diary which have definitions are printed in **bold** and these appear in alphabetical order in the glossary. It is hoped that the glossary will provide a useful starting point for the understanding of local history, so that readers may be encouraged to read and research further into what can be a fascinating study.

Appendices

These include several relevant family trees, transcripts of wills, inventories and other documents thought to be of interest.

The Bibliography

To encourage further research there is an extensive reading list which contains most of the books and papers that were used, divided into subjects. Please remember that new ideas are constantly updating our knowledge of local history so this list cannot be considered exhaustive.

Acknowledgements

My thanks are due to the many people who took part in this project. First and foremost to the late Peter Pownall who took the trouble to write his diary for us to read. To Mrs Ann Bayliss who found a reference to the diary and who drew it to the attention of David Reid, then Head of the Stockport Library Study Room. To David Reid who obtained a copy of the diary from The University of Reading Archives & Manuscripts Department and gave it to me to look at.

Thanks also to those members of my class who transcribed and typed the first copy of the diary and who include Mrs Sylvia Callow, Mr Conrad Frost, Mrs Hazel Godley, Mrs Fiona Graham, Mrs Sylvia Hill, Mrs Ann Hutchfield, Mrs Gill Jackson, Mrs Fran Platt, Mrs Wendy Robinson, Mrs Gwynneth Stringer, Mrs Grace Smith, Mrs Helen Sugden and Mrs Rosemary Watkins. The research for the glossary was started in class but was continued afterwards by a small group named below. Conrad Frost, whose love of detail led him to copy out local records and start the index; Wendy Robinson, who painstakingly traced the family histories; Helen Sugden who researched many of the agricultural references; and Rosemary Watkins who delighted in the social practices of the period.

Very special thanks are due to Wendy Robinson whose research, work on compiling the bibliography, and painstaking checking and re-checking, along with her unflagging faith gave me the support I needed throughout the whole project.

My thanks too to Sylvia Hill who typed and retyped the material; to my husband, Angus, who helped me to put it all onto computer, and prepared it for printing; to Fiona Graham and Fran Platt for checking the diary transcripts; and to all the others who took an interest and encouraged us. No thanks can repay the hours of work and enthusiasm everyone put in.

I am greatly indebted to Mr Paul Booth, MA, of the Department of Further Education, Liverpool University, who helped with many definitions, especially those relating to the Poor Law, Government Acts, Cheshire history and the various judicial courts, who read the entire work, and gave much useful advice and encouragement along the way. Also to the staffs of the Cheshire Record Office, where I consulted the mss for Bramhall manor, the Poor Law and the Pownall family; John Rylands University Library, Deansgate, Manchester for papers relating to Bramhall and Norbury; Manchester Library, Local History department, for newspaper records and local history; and most of all Stockport Central Library, Study Room, where we consulted local history records.

Finally my grateful thanks to the publishers, the Stockport Historical Society and Old Vicarage Publications, for making a dream come true. All proceeds from the sale of this book will go to the Society's publication fund.

Heather Coutie   July 1989

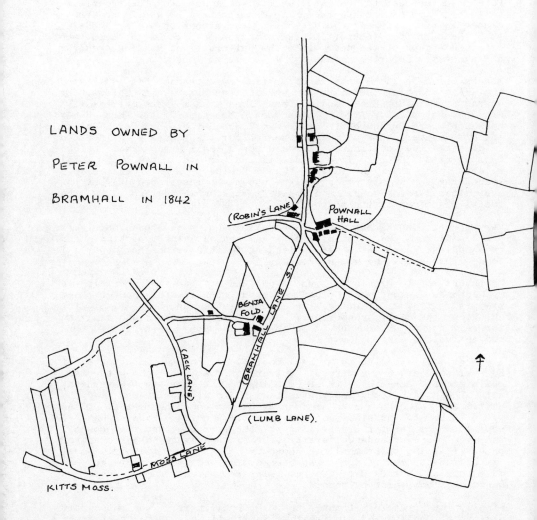

LANDS OWNED BY

PETER POWNALL IN

BRAMHALL IN 1842

CONTENTS

TRANSCRIPT OF THE DIARY OF PETER POWNALL OF BRAMHALL, 1782-1789

Photocopy of the first entries in the Diary

Transcript of the Diary

1782	October	
4th [Fri]	Finished **Leading Wheat, Meal** 33s p[er] **Load**	Diary
5	Begun to lead **Oats, Malt** 40s p[er] Load	p 1
7	Got done **Shearing**	
8	Mr Clark of Stockport was **killed** by a **horse**	
8	Miss **Birch** died	
10	**Old Michealmas Day**, Fetched 3 **heifers** and	
	1 **Colt** out of **Poynton Lay**, 50 **Sheep** enter	
	ed into Grass	
11	Mr Clark and Miss Birch were interred	
12	Got done leading **Corn Meal** 32 p[er] L[oad]	
14	Mr George **Hulme** went to Oxford	
14	Begun to get up **pottatoes** for keeping	
14	Paid Wm **Hallworth** one **Highway Lay**	
	for the year 1782 value £1 12s 9d	

DIARY

1782	October	
15th	**Marked Sheep** with P. on the further side	Diary
15	James Prestnal fetched his **Cow** out of	p 2
	our Lay. 16 killed a young **Rabit** first	
	this Season	
17	Ann Pot took her Cow out of our Lay and	
	entered her with our Cows into the **Eddish**	
	at 2s per week	
17	Killed two hives of **bees**	
18	Mr George **Worthington** went off for London	
18	**Hanged** Pharoah & Phillis, Meal 30s	
19	Paid Joseph Clark one **Constable Lay**	
	Value 8s 2d	
20	Mr **Brocklehurst** preached a funeral	
	Sermon occasioned by the Death of	
	Miss Birch his tex was Psalm 90th 12 vs	

1782	October	
21	Mrs Martha Lockwood died after a Short illness	Diary
23	**Stockport fair**. Got done Getting Pottatoes	p 3
24	**Holed** Pottatoes	
25	Sold Mr Worthington 3 Load of Pottatoes	
	Meal 35s per Load	
26	Covered the **Asparagus** to preserve it from the	
	frost	
26	Malt 45s per Load	
28	Thomas **Roads** Houshold goods sold	
31	Sister wrote to my aunt Blunt	

1782	November	
1st [Fri]	Meal 36s per Load	
3	Mr Brocklehurst adminestered the Sacrament	
4	Thomas Shacroft was [?] **Burriid** and died of it	
5	Mr **Hulme** and Father went to Lostock a **courseing**	
	killed no **hare**	
6	Sister went to Mr Brocklehurst's	
7	A Meeting at John **Glaves** concerning Robe	

1782	November	
8th	Meal 35s per load, Mary **Benison** was	Diary
	delivered of a Daughter	p 4
9th	**Laid Cows in** the **Shippen**	
9	Father Shot a **Woodcock** First	
11	New **Martinmas Day**	
12	Drawed Pottatoes Ground into **Buts**	
13	Begun a Ploughing **Barley** Ground	
	for to sow wheat upon it	
14	Miss Hulme Miss Lockwood & Miss	
	Nancy Hulme drank **Tea** at our house	
14	**Thatched bee Hives**	

2

15	Meal 34 per Load
16	Malt £2 2s per Load
18	**Manchester fair** called Dirt Fair

1782   **November**

19th	Mr & Mrs **Davenport** went to **Bury St Edman's**	Diary
20	Mr Joshua **Killer** & Mr George Killer came to our house	p 5
21th	Begun a **sowing** wheat	
22	Old Martinmas Day	
22	Altringham **fair**, Meal 36s per Load	
23	Malt 44s per Load, Flower 48s per Load	
22	Gave Over making **cheese**	
25	Mr Joshua & Mr G Killer went to Nottingham	
25	Begun a **phallowing**	
26	Laid in the Horse's	
27	John Hallworth died	

1782 .   **December**

4th [Wed]	Sent Mr Worthington & Mr Harrop each a **Turky**	Diary
4th	Received one Load of **Carrots** at 5s 10d	p 6
5	**Bramhall Court**	
6	Got a new Diary	
7	Meal 37s per Load	
8	Mr John Birch came to our house	
11	**Cheadle Hulme Court**	
13	Meal 38s per Load	
13	George Fildes fetched the last **Ewe**	
14	Mr Hulme and I went a courseing into Stya[l] killed one Hare	
16	Mr Barton and I went a courseing into Woodford	

1782   **December**

17th	Mr Leigh sent my Father notice to keep off Woodford; dated 14th of December	Diary
18	Betty Miller paid £2 for **rent**	p 7
18	Sold William Bennison one Load of Meal at 36s per Load	
19	Henry Taylor laid one of his Horese's	
20	Paid Mrs Hays £1 5s for Pownall Mottram's Board	
20	Got done sowing Wheat	
20	Mr G Hulme came down from Oxford	
21	Fetched ten new **Mahagony Chairs** from Manchester	
22	Sent Mr Brocklehurst a Turkey	
24	Christmas Eve	

1782		December	
25		New Christmas Day	Diary
25		A Meetting at James **Goldens** for the settleing of John Halworth's Lays	p 8
26		Killed two **Pigs**	
26		Finished Phallawing	
26		Sent Mr John Worthington a Turky	
27		Sent Mr. Walker half a Pig	
27		Meal 34s 6d per Load	

1783		January	
1s	[Wed]	Gave Pownall Mottram £1 1s	Diary
1		Father Received of Mr Richard Bancroft £236 17s 6	p 9
1		Father received of Joseph Wood ten Guineas of the **Principal** Sixty three Pounds	
3		Meal 36s Per Load	
4		John Brown paid Twenty eight pounds being the first half year's rent due Martinmas 1782	
5		Mr Brocklehurst adminestered the Sacrament	
6		Joshua Shaw took his calf out our Winter Lay	
7		Black Cow **calved** First this year	
10		Meal 36s per Load	
11		**Tithe** Day held at James Golden on **Bramhal Green**	

1783		January	
12		Sister went to Mr Worthington's	Diary
13		Miss Wright was married to Mr Price a Walch Gentleman	p 10
14		Sold Mr John Wood a peice of Land in **Marple** for a road to his house	
17th		Paid Mr **Watson Rector** Bramhall tithe	
18		Mr Hallworth's ware House burn'd	
22		A Meeting at John Glave's concerning Settleing the tithe	
23		Rebecca Hulme died aged 89 Years	
24		Meal 37s per Load	
27th		Rebecca Hulme Buried	
27		Killed a **Partraige** First	
31		Sold Cheese at £2. 2s per Hundred weight	

1783		February	
1	[Sat]	James **Dooly** begun his **Eleven months**	Diary
3		Begun of nailing up the [?] **Wall Trees**	p 11
5		Weighed our Cheese to 19C	
8		Took our Cheese to Robert **Haveyard**	
13		Sent two Men and a Team to repair the **Highways** 1 Day 1783	
17		Begun a ploughing for Oats	
22		**Geese** begun a Laying	

4

1783   **March**

4 [Tues]   Shrove Tuesday
5   Sister and Mother went to Manchester to
              buy **Wedding Cloth's** and devided Miss
              Birch's Cloth's
              Killed tow Pigs

1783   **March**

8   Sent 35 Measures of Barly to **Deanrow** in   Diary
              order to be made into Malt   p 12
11th   Got done ploughing Lay Grounds
11   Begun to ploughing **Stuble** Grounds
12s   Begun a diging for **peas**
14   John Watson Rector of Stockport died
14   Set peas
14   Bought two **store pigs**
15   **Set Geese**
17   Sold Robert Hambleton a Mare
18   Joseph **Shaw** disembodied from the **Militia**
18   .   **Set Beans**

1783   **March**

22   Got a New **Carpet**   Diary
25   Got in Pottatoes   p 13
25   Stockport fair
27   **Sister Sarah** married Mr John Brocklehurst
              of Macclesfield
27   Fetched Malt from Deanrow **kill**
28   Got done **thrashing** Oats

1783   **April**

7 [Mon]   Sowed Carrots   Diary
7   Sheep Men fetched their **Whinterers**   p 14
8   Sowed Onions, Lettice's Celery, Savoy's
              and Radishes, Transplanted Cabage's
10   Sowed Colliflower Seed
12   Begun a ploughing barly Grownd **Cross**
18   Good Friday
21   **Castrated** a Colt
24   Tryed Jereboam Williamson's **residenc**
              [A]t [?Salford]

1783   **June**

3 [Tues]   George Hulme Married to Sarah Partington   Diary
5   Joseph Shaw & Jenny Glave Married   p 15
9   Whitsun Monday
10   Begun a makeing **Summer Work**
15   Sister Brocklehurst made Her **Appearance**

19	at Dean row Got Done makeing summerwork	
23	**Barnaby fair**	
25	begun a limeing	
30	Begun to fetch Lime from the Kill	
30	of June Mondy Thomas Pecken. (?) Gone came to our Hous	
25	Trusted Robert Hamleston one sack of Oats at 40 shillings P.S. [entry deleted with two crosses] Oats at 40 shillings P.S.	

1783   **July**

4	[Fri]	Last Calf went	Diary p 16
6		Ann Haywood came to live at our house	
8		Sent ten Sixteen scores of Wheat to Altringham	
10		Began to gather **Moor Lays**	
13		**Presbury Wakes**	
14		Begun a **Mowing**	
15		Begun a Leading Hay	
26		**Old Swithin's day**	
29		Knutsford **Races** three Days	

1783   **August**

1	[Fri]	Got done Mowing
2		New meal at Mnchester
5		Got done **Haying**
6		Begun a **mucking** Meadows

1783   **August**

7	Old Phillip **Fallows** married	Diary p 17
8	Tithe Day held at Dog and Partrige in Stockport	
14	Begun a Shearing	
20	Sent Mr Brocklehurst half a'Load of Wheat	
23	Begun to draw summer work into Butts	
23	Norbury **Wakes**	
23	Begun a Leading Corn	
29	Mr Harrop **inocalated** his four Children	

September

11	[Tues]	John Glave got a **Licience** to sell Ale
17		Got done Shearing
24		Got done Ladeing Corn
25		Begun a sowing Wheat

1783	September	
25	Went a courseing into Mottram	Diary
	Killed a **Lease** of Hares	p 18
26	James Preistnal shot a Hare	
29	New Michealmas Day	
23[sic]	Mr Whitney was married to Miss Wardle	

1783	August [deleted] October	
2 [Thur]	Got done sowing Wheat	
7	**Macclesfield Races** four Days	
9	Fifty sheep came into our Lay	
11	Old Michealmas Day	
11	Fetched two heifers & a colt out of **Pointon Park**	
12	Mr Whitney & his Lady made their appearance at Deanrow	
12	Bought half a score of Ewes	
11	Begun a getting Pottatoes	

1783	October	
14	Sent Mr Brocklehurst a Couple of Turkies	Diary
14	**Docked** two Colts	p 19
18	William Benison's **Fairing**	
18	Begun a threshing Oats	
17	William Armatage & William Halworth put on to be **Overseers of the Highways**	
21	Thomas fallows & William Armatage chosen constables	
22	Slip gooseberry and Currant Trees	
23	Stockport Fair	
25	Set Cabbage Plants	
30	Killed a Woodcock	

1783	November	
3 [Mon]	Begun a mucking for Barly	
3	Mary Brown came to **live** at our house	
4	Killed a hair in Bramhall	
5	Mother & Father went to Macklesfied	

1783	November	
10	Gave over makeing Cheese	Diary
11	New Martinmas Day	p 20
11	Begun a phallowing	
14	Laid cows in	
18	Set Marple **Estate**	
18	Got done phallowing	
19	Docked White foot	
19	Killed two Pigs	

17	Settled with Joshua Shaw	
21	Father Paid his tithe	
21	Sold Cheese at £2 2s per C[wt]	
22	Old Martimas Day	
27	Brother William begun **accompts**	
27	Mary Benison deliverd of Boy	

1783 December

2 [Tues]	Edmund Massey married Hannah Bracegirdle	Diary p 21
4	Cheadle Hulme Court	
4	John Williamson of Woodford sold up	
5	Begun a selling Meal	
9	Bramhall Court	
11	John Bullock married Mary Pownall	
23	Laid the Horses in	
24	Christmas Eve	
24	Bought a **Liceince for Carts**	
29	First Cow calfed	

1784 January

1 [Thurs]	John Brown Paid his rent	Diary p 22
9	Sent Mr Broklehurst a Turkey	

February

2 [Mon]	New **Candlemas Day** Sister Mary begun Accoumpts
4	Sold First calf
7	Joseph Birch married to Miss Skippin
9	John Houlme and I went a courseing into Woodford and Killed two Hares
12	Old Candlemas Day
15	John Marsland died
18	3 Sheep Worried
20	Sister Broklehurst delivered of a Boy at 11 o'Clock A.M.

1784 January [deleted] February

26	Mr **Preistnall** weighted our Cheese	Diary p 23
29	Geese begun a laying	
27	Begun a ploughing	

1784 March

3 [Wed]	Stockport fair
6	Thomas Bayly came to live at our House
13	Sent Cheese into the Market
13	Bought two store pigs

14	Sent 32 measures of Barly to the Malt Kiln	
16	Got done threshing oats	
19	Set Geese	
20	Set Peas & Beans	
25	Stockport fair	
27	Made **Birch wine**	
31	First Ewe Lambed	

1784   **April**

1 [Thurs]	Begun ploughing Barly Ground	Diary
2	Got lime and soil away	p 24
3	Fetched Malt Home	
3	Sowed Carrots, Lettece's, & Radishs	
5	Begun a sowing Oats	
6	Sowed Onions	
8	Set Potatoes	
8	Bought two store Pigs	
[1]2	**School Master** gave over teaching School	
[1]3	Mr Brocklehurst Baptized his Child William	
[1]9	Good Friday	
19	Thomas Bayley begun to live at our House at 1s per week and to stay til Christmas	

1784   **April**

23	Father went off **Overseer of the poor** Samuel Clark succeeded him	Diary p 25
28	Presbury fair	
29	Got done sowing Oat	
30	Begun a sowing Barly	

1784   **May**

1 [Sat]	New May day	
1	Stockport fair	
3	Begun a making **Potatoes Bows**	
4	Sister Brocklehurst came to our house the first time since her lying in	
10	Set potatoes	
12	Old may day, Sent three **twinters** and a Calf	
12	Laid Cows Out	
12	Got done sowing Barly	

1784   **May**

12	Begun to make[ing deleted] Cheese	Diary
18	Took a Colt to Robert Bennet Lay in Derbyshire	p 26
21	Begun a fetching lime from the Kiln	
22	Begun a making summer-work	
25	**Washed Sheep**	
25	Mr **Prescott** was married to Miss Dyson	

DIARY

28	Sheered sheep
31	Transplanted Colifowers & Savoy-Cabbage
31	Begun a weeding Corn

1784   **June**

9	[Wed]	Begun a going to the Highway
9		Sold the **Lambs**
19		Got done making Summer work
22		Barnaby fair
25		Bees swarmed
30		Ploughed Potatoes
30		Got done weeding corn

1784   **July**

5	[Mon]	Begun a mowing
7		Begun a crossing summer Work
8		Transplanted winter Greens
9		Begun a leading Hay
11		Presbury wakes
12		Woodford Races
13		Bromhall Court
17		Lambs clear'd off
21		Sister Alice went to Manchester to school
22		Begun a **manureing** the Meadows
27		Knutsford Races 3 Days
30		Thomas Pickford Sold a Cow
30		Got done mowing

Diary
p 27

1784   **August**

2	[Mon]	Went into Derbyshire a looking Colt
4		Plucked Geese
3		Got done Leading hay
6		Got done Seling Meal
6		Mrs Killer died
9		Sowed Cabbage seed
12		Went to the Moors a shooting
16		Brother William went to school
19		Harrowed summerwork
23		Went into Poynton park a looking Cattle [illegible]
24		Drawed summerwork into Buts
27		Begun a Sheering

Diary
p 28

1784   **September**

8	[Wed]	Begun a Leading corn
18		Mr and Mrs **Murry** came to our House
25		Got done sheering
27		Sheep cleared off
29		New Michealmas Day

Diary
p 29

1784   **October**

1	[Fri]	Begun a sowing wheat
7		Got done Leading Corn
6		Killed a hare
8		40 sheep came into our Lay
9		Paid William Hallworth Highway Lays
10		Old Michealmas Day
11		Fetched 3 **Stirks** and 1 Calf out of Poynton
12		Fetched Colt out of Darbyshire
12		Went a coursing into Mottram Killed 5 Hares

1784   **October**

13	Begun a Getting Potatoes up
11	Got a **Licience for one Horse**
13	John Hallworth and Richard Phallows came on to be overseers of the Highways
15	Mr George Birch came to our House
15	George Fields died
19	Got done geting Potatoes up
20	Settled with Martha Fieldes
21	Cover'd the Asparugus
23	Stockport fair
25	Bought a **score** of Ewes
27	Begun a threshing oats
29	Killed a woodcock

Diary
p 30

1784   **November**

11	[Thurs]	New Martinmas Day
12		Laid Cows in
12		Sold **Bay mare**
16		Begun a Phallowing
19		Paid tithe
22		Old Martinmas Day
26		Got done Phallowing

Diary
p 31

1784   **December**

2	[Thurs]	Bramhall Court
3		Gave over makeing cheese
7		Laid the Horses in
10		Begun a selling meal
17		Brother William came home from School
21		Sister Ally came from school

1784   **December**

24	Sold two Pigs
25	Christmas Day
28	Philip Fallow's wife Died of Child Bed
31	Thomas Golden Paid his First halfyears rent

Diary
p 32

31   Thomas Goulden Paid his first half years rent

1785   **January**

3 [Mon]   William Baylay came to live at our House for a
year but a week his wages is 7 Guineas for a
11 Months
6   Mother went to Stockport to prove Mrs Killer
will 6 Janry. Sent Mr Hardy [£12.12s deleted]
7   Bought 4 Store Pigs
9   First Cow calved
18   Killed a Pig
24   Peter Pownall Exchanged a **Moss room**

1785   **January**

               lying on the North side of **Kits Moss** with   Diary
Robert Hardy for one lying on the East   p 33
Side of Kits Moss called the Moss Pits

1785   **February**

1 [Tues]   Peter Pownall was served with a **summons**
form Mr Wright to show the reason he did
[he did deleted] not pay the the mony he had
in his hands at the Expiration of his Office
8   Shrove tuesday
8   Sent Barly 30 Measures to the Malt Kill at
Deanrow
11   Goose begun a laying
12   Peter Pownall & Robert Hardy went to
[Wilm deleted] Wimslow
15   Begun a plowing
14   Set Marple Estate to Joseph Moors for
£[illegible]

1785   **March**

7 [Mon]   Went to Chappel in le frith with George   Diary
Worthington to pay £10-0-0 Advanced on an   p 34
Estate lying in Chinly in Glossop Parish
known by the name of Hull also another at
bowden head in the parish of Chappel
in le frith both in Derbyshire
11   Mrs Shaw of Altringham died
17   Mrs Davenport, Miss Richmond & two Miss
Crips drank tea
17   Set peas
19   Set Beans
22   Transplanted Cabbage Plants
24   Sowed Onions Carrats & Lettices
25   New Lady Day: Stockport fair
26   Went to Manchester to buy iron for [?] **Strikes**

1785   **April**

2	[Sat]	Fetched Malt home	Diary
4		Got done ploughing for Oats	p 35
5		Begun a sowing Oats	
5		Old Lady Day	
9		Set Potatoes sowd Redish seed	
9		Got done sowing Oats	
22		Set potatoes	
22		Sowed Barly	
27		Sold Cheese at 40s per C[wt]	
30		Sowed Cucumber seed	
30		Begun a makeing Chees	
30		Begun a going to the Highway	

1785   **May**

12	[Thurs]	Old May day sent 1 Stirk & 1 Calf to	Diary
		Poynton Park	p 36
14		Laid Cows out	
14		Sold the Ewes & Lambs to William Hudson	
15		Mr Brocklehurst began a **Catichising**	
14		Mr B jun[io]r inoculated his son William	
18		**Manchester Races**	
27		Begun a fetching lime from the Kill	

          June

15	[Wed]	Begun a weeding Corn
14		James Hough came to Live at our house
14		Two Miss Brocklehurst of Mottram came to our house to stay a few nights
22		Barnaby Fair
27		Begun a mowing **Clover**
29		Sent Mr Hardy 20£ [deleted with two crosses]

1785   **July**

4	[Mon]	Begun a Leading Clover	Diary
8		Begun a mowing hay grass	p 37
11		Begun a Laiding hay	
16		Got done mowing	
20		Bramhall Court	
27		William Pownall went to **Stand School**	
29		Knutsford Races	
30		Begun a mucking Meadows	

1785   **August**

8	[Mon]	Sowed Cabbage seed
8		Begun a shearing
11		Went to the **Play**
12		Went a moor game shooting

14	John Priestnall of **Witford** Died	
29	Begun a leading Corn	

1785   **September**

10 [Sat]	Mowed the second crop of **clover**	Diary
15	Got done shearing	p 38
20	Mr J: Dale of Stockport Buried his youngest son	
21	**Grand Festival of Musick** at Manchester for 3 Days	
29	New Mickealmas Day	

1785   **Aug October**

3 [Wed]	Got done Leading Corn
3	Transplant'd Cabbage Plants
4	**Knutsford sessions**
4	Mr Brocklehurst and I went to stand to see William Pownall
6	31 Lambs came to winter
8	Covered the Asparagus
10	Michealmas Day Old

1785   **October**

14 [Fri]	Joshua Shaw died	Diary
18	Begun agetting Potatoes	p 39
24	Stockport fair	

[1785]   **November**

1 [Tues]	Benjamin Pownall died
2	George Hulme paid his Niece Jane Pownall **Fortune £400**
4	**Mr Pickfords Cotten Shop** Broke in Poynton
8	Begun ploughing clover root for wheat
9	Begun a sowing wheat
14	Laid the cows in
15	Cheadle Hulme Court
21	Gave over makeing Cheese
22	Begun a phallowing
23	Got done sowing wheat
25	Paid tithe

1785   **November**

23	Mr Meldrum **Desenting** Minester married to Miss J Alcock of Gatley	Diary p 40

1785   **December**

1	[Thur]	Bramhall Court
5		Mrs Harrop of Altringham died of childbed
7		Laid in the Horses
25		William Pownall came form [sic] school
		New Christmas Day

	£	s	d
2 Ld Pottatoes p[er] 18d	1	6	0
Cash		12	0
6 peck meal 3/5	1	1	0
3 Tubs Coal at 7/2		1	10

	3	0	10

	s	
1 pk Meal	4	0
1 D potato	1	1
Cash	3	0

	8	1
		10

	8	11

1786   **January**

9	[Mon]	James Burgess came to live at our House	Diary
20		**Benison's Place** sold 264£ at Mr Taylor's	p 41
		in the Hilgate Stockport
23		William Pownall went to stand school
24		Begun to plough for **Vetches**
29		Went to Altrincgham a Courseing

[1786]   **February**

1	[Wed]	Mr George Worthington was married to a
		Miss Fanny Russel of Birmingham
3		Alice Pownall went to Macclesfield
7		Began to plough for Oats
10		Sold Cheese at 22s for 1 C[wt] : 15 C
10		Bought a pig to feed
27		Shrove Tuesday
27		James Burgess Married to [blank]

1786   **March**

19	[Sun]	George Killer died	Diary
21		Went to Mottram a Valueing **Timber**	p 42
24		Sold Timber to William Jackson
25		New Lady Day
28		Sowed Lettice Radishes
31		- Onions & Carrots
31		Paid **Dowray** left by John Pownall to Mary
		Bullock £20

DIARY

1786		April
4	[Tues]	Sowed Vetches
		Begun sowing Oats
5		Old Lady Day
3		Elizabeth Pownall married
12		Sowed Parsley seed
14		Good Friday

1786	April	
21	Uncovered the Asparagus	Diary
22	Got done sowing Oats	p 43
24	Set Cabbage plants	
25	- Kidney beans	
29	- Asparagus seed	
27	Lawrence Kilner married to Jane Hulme	

1786		May
7	[Sun]	Set Potatoes [Easter Sunday]
9		Sowed Cucumber Seed
12		Laid Cows out
16		Sowed Barley
20		Begun to sell Milk
23		Laid horses to grass
24		Begun to maki[ng deleted] summerwork

1786	June	
1	[Thurs] Bess foaled	Diary
1	Mother and sisters drank tea at Bramhall Hall	p 44
14	Transplanted Colleflowr plants	
20	Do Brockily Savoys Cabbage Celery Plants	
22	**Barnaby** faire	
23	William Pownall came from school	
27	Got Peas	

1786		July
3	[Mon]	Sowed turnip seed
3		ploughed up Potatoes
6		Begun ploughing summer work
4		Mr John Collier Grocer in Stockport married
6		Begun a mowing
13		Do Leading hay
21		Got done mowing
26		Got done Leading Hay
27		Harrow'd Summer work

[Pages 44 & 45 are overlaid with accounts, an example of which is reproduced in Appendix I]

16

1786	July	
29	Drawed summer work into Butts	Diary
31	[Line deleted]	p 45

1786	August	
4 [Fri]	Mrs Brocklehurst deliverd of a Daughter 11 O.clock A.M.	
4	Mowed Vetches	
4	Manured the further Bank	
7	William Pownall Went to Stand school	

1786*	June	
1*	Bess foaled	Diary
1*	Mother and sisters drank tea at Bramhall Hall	p 46

[* deleted in original diary; remainder of page contains accounts of John Redfern's wages]

1786	July	
29	Drawed summer work in to butts	Diary
31	[Line deleted]	p 47

1786	August	
4 [Fri]	Mrs Brocklehurst brought to bed of a Girl 11 O.Clock A.M.	
4	Mowed Vetches	
4	Manured the further Bank	
7	William Pownall went to stand school	
11	Took a **licience to kill Game**	
12	Went a moor Game shootting	
17	Got **sluch** out of the watering Pool	
19	Revd William Brocklehurst died of Leigh hall and Minister of deanrow Chapel	
21	Begun a Sheiring	
22	Revd William Brocklehurst Intered	
25	Took the tithe	

1786	September	
3 [Sun]	Revd William Brocklehurst Funeral Sermon preached at Deanrow by Mr Mainly his Text was Ecclesiastes Vll 2,3,4, verses	Diary p 48
3	**Wilmslow wakes**	
15 [overwritten 17]	Paid Lawrence Walkers Bill for **shewing** James Goulden	
17	Begun a leading Corn	

17

19	Mowed second crop clover	
21	Got done shearing	
20	Turned cows into Eddish	
23	John Hugh & Lidia Leah married	
29	New Michealmas Day	

1786   **October**

2 [Mon]	Got done Leading corn	
3	Got in Clover	
5	Wained Colt	
	48 Sheep came to winter	
6	Begun to sow wheat	
10	Old Michealmas Day	

1786   **October**

11	Bought two heifers of Mr Hardy	Diary
15	Mr Chadwick chosen minister of deanrow	p 49
19	Got done sowing wheat	
21	_____ getting potatoes	
27	Mr & Mrs Davenport drank tea at our house	

1786   **November**

1 [Wed]	Coverd the Asparaguss	
10	Set cabbage plants	
11	New Martinmas Day	
13	Begun a phallowing for Oats	
14	_____ for turnips	
15	Laid in the cows	
16	Begun a thrashing oats	
17	Paid the tithe	
22	Old Martinmas day	

1786   **October [sic]**

5	Subscribed to the **Manchester Acadamy** £2.2.	
8	Laid in the Horses	

1786   **December**

21 [Thurs]	William Pownall came from school	Diary
22	[Illegible]	p 50
25	New Christmas Day	
4	Bramhall Court	
30	John **Arden** Esqr of Stockport died	

[1787]   **January**

1 [Mon]	Settled with Mr Worthington of Altringm	

2	James Pownall came to live at our house
	Received of Edmund Massey Willm Jackson
	& Daniel Massey 105£ being one half of
	the **Timber** Mony
6	John Arden Esqr of Stockport Intered
10	Set peas
11	Mr Pope came to our house
12	Began to sell Meal
11	Killed a pig which was [?] **M-z-t-d**
18	**Inclosed** a piece of Ground on the Common
19	Paid Mr Worthingtons Bill

1787　　　　**January**

15	paid William Pownall 50£ being a Legacy	Diary
	Left by J. Powne[ll]	p 51
22	[Deleted]	
23	Began to plough for Oats	
25	Measured 3 Acres of Land in Cheadle Hulme	
	left to a school in that Township by Jonathan	
	Robersons of Stockport for ever	

[1787]　　　　**February**

2	[Fri]	Candlemas day
3		Miss Pownall went to Mr Worthingtons to
		go to the **Stockport Assembley**
9		George Hulme of Lindow died
11		Went to **stockport Chapel**
15		Revd George Birch married to Miss Jane
		Taylor of Manchester
24		Set Beans

[1787]　　　　**March**

3	[Sat]	Alice Pownall went to Mr Worthingtons to
		go to the [Stockport Assembly]

1787　　　　**March**

5	Stockport fair	Diary
10	Mr Lingard paid [?] 56£ being Interest	p 52
13	Went to Altringham	
14	Began sowing Oats & Set Potatoes	
15	sowed Colliflower seed	
17	Mrs Clark of stockport died suddenly	
20 [or 22]	William Pownall went to school	
23	Sowed Onions & Carrots	
25	Lady Day New	
26	Stockport Fair	
30	Transplanted Coliflower	
31	Sowed Radish's & Lettice's	

DIARY

[1787]	April	
5 [Thurs]	Lady day Old	
12	Got done sowing Oats	
13	sowed Barley	
[?] 17	_____ Vetches	

1787   **April**

14	Uncovered the Asparagus	Diary
21	Set potatoes	p 53
25	sowed clover seed & **Trefoil** in little Balgrave	
-	Made an asparagus Bed and planted it	
-	sowed **yellow Turnip** seed	

[1787]   **May**

1 [Tues]	Stockport fair
5	Set kidney Beans
7	Ploughed the Turnip Ground cross
8	sowed cucumber seed
11	Sarah Marslands resedenc tryed at Stockport she is made a Bramhall woman
12	Old May Day
14	Laid the Cow's to Grass
15	Went to **Liverpool** along with Mr Tho Worthing[ton] a Journey of plasure
16	Bess foaled
17	Returned from Liverpool
	Sent a colt to a Lay in Derbyshire

1787   **May**

16	Begun a selling **Milk**	Diary
20	Mr Chadwick began to catichise	p 54
21	Began to fetch lime from **how Lane** and set in sow field	
23	Fished Brook	
28	Whit Munday	
29	Transplanted coliflower plants	
30	Paid Jonathan Dickinson being the Last of his share of a fourth part of 163£	
-	Manchester races began	
31	Plowed pottatoes rows up	

[1787]   **June**

11 [Mon]	Begun a limeing straight field
13	Alice Pownal went to Macclesfield
14	Mucked for turnips
15	Sowed Turnips
15	Transplanted lettices
16	Turned horse to Grass

1787		June	
16		Mr Davenport Drank tea at our house	Diary
12		Day of sail of Richard fallows Good & Chattels	p 55
18		Transplanted Winter Grane & [? Savoy] plants Wm Pownall came from Stand school	
22		Barnaby fair	
23		[entry deleted]	
27		ploughed pottatoes rows up	
26		Get pottatoes	
28		Sowed Turnips 2[n]d time	
		Sowed Turnips 2[n]d time	

[1787]		July	
6	[Fri]	James Pownall was killed by a horse	
6		Sowed Turnips 3 [rd] time	
7		[entry deleted]	
8		The Jury sat on the Body of Jas Pownall and gave in their Verdict that he was accidentlly killed by a horse passing over him	

1787		July	
6		Began a Mowing	Diary
12		Bramhall Court	p 56
14		Sowed Turnips fourth & Last Time	
15		Presbury Wakes	
11		Daniel Massey paid 105£ being the remaing part of Timber Mony sold in Mottram &c	
19		Began a leading hay	
29		Paid half years **salery** for a seat in Dean Row Chapel	
31		Knutsford Races	
31		Wm Pownall went to school to Wilson Stockport	

[1787]		August	
2	[Thurs]	Went to Knutsford Races	
6		Got done Mowing	
9		Got done leading hay	
12		Went to moor Game shooting killed a Brace	
13		Got done howing Turnips	
19		Marshall Killer came to Bramhall	
17		Got done selling Meal	
22		Began a shearing	
24		Mowed Vetches	
30		Mrs Davenport drank tea at our house	

1787		September	
2	[Sun]	Wilmslow wakes	Diary
7		Began a leading Corn	p 57

10	Miss Francis Brocklehurst died
12	_____ Buried
10	Orrotory of Musick at **Stockport Old Church**
15	Got done shearing
20	Began a sowing wheat
24	Got done Leading corn
23	A funeral sermon at dean row Occasioned by the Death of Miss Francis Brocklehurst Test 1 Chrons 29 chap 15 Verse Latter part
29	New Michal day
-	Turned cows into **Eddish**

[1787]   **October**

5 [Fri]	Wained colt
10	Michaelmas day Old fetched two heifers from lay
-	40 sheep came to winter
11	Fetched a colt out of derbyshire
12	Began to get Potatoes

1787   **October**

| 22 | Transplanted Cabbage Plants | Diary |
| 23 | Stockport Fair | p 58 |

1787   **November**

3 [Sat]	Got done getting Pottatoes
6	Began to Get Turnips for Cows
7	Covered the asparaguss
9	Laid in Cows
11	New Martinmas Day
11	Bro[the]r & Sis[te]r Brocklehurst received sacrament
15	Mr B inoculated his daughter
18	Miss Bro[ckle]hurst rec[eive]d sacrament
22	Old Martinmas Day
30	Paid tithe

1787   **December**

3 [Mon]	Bramhall Court
4	Began a phallowing
22	William [line deleted]

1788   **January**

| 1 [Tues] | Set Peas | Diary |
| 2[?] | William Pownall returned to school | p 59 |

22

1788		**February**	
2	[Sat]	Candlemas New	
9		Went a coursing to Dunham	
9		Mrs Mary Hardy died	
		Candlemas Old	
14		Two Miss Grimshaws Mr & Mrs W[orthing]ton & Mrs Hardy dined drank tea	
18		Drank tea and spent Evening at Mrs Hardys Stockport	
19		Stockport Assembly	
20		Began a plowing for Oats	
25		Set Beans	

1788		**March**	
1	[Sat]	Transplanted coliflowers & cabbages	
4		Stockport fair	
17		Sowed Coliflower seed	
15		Went to Gorton drank tea	
22		Sowed Raddishes & Lettice	
24	.	**Mr Banks** began a course of lectures at Stockport	
24		[illegible]	

1788		**April**	
3	[Thurs]	Got done ploughing for Oats	Diary
4		Began a sowing Oats	p 60
5		Lady Day Old	
17		Got done sowing Oats	
8		Set potatoes	
18		___ Beans second Crop	
22		Unovered the Asparagus	

1788		**May**	
1	[Thurs]	Stockport fair	
3		Mr Robert **Grimshaw** of Gorton died	
-		Went to Manchester	
11		Whitsunday	
12		Old May Day Turned Cows into Grass	
13		Set potatoes	
16		Sowed Cucumber seed	
17		Took 2 colts to a Lay in Derbyshire	

1788	**May**	
8	Mr Mather & Miss Brocklehurst married	Diary
		p 61

DIARY

1788	June
3 [Tues]	Turned horse to Grass
19[?]	Sowed Turnips first time
21	Barnaby fair
22	Sowed Turnips 2[n]d Time
-	Transplanted Brockley, Savoys, Coliflowers
17	Began a Mowing Ryegrass

1788	July
15 [Tues]	Old swithin
-	Bramhall Court
16	Began to hoe Turnips
22	Began a Mowing Grass
28	- Leading hay
31	Went to Knutsford Races

1788	August
4 [Mon]	Got done mowing

1788	August
5	Got done leading hay
9	Begun a Sheering
12	Went a Moor game Shooting
15	Mrs Murray died

Diary
p 62

1788	September
2 [Tues]	Got done shearing
9	Got done Leading corn
10	Sister Alice came from Altringham
23	William Pownall - - - [illegible]
29	Michealmas Day new

1788	October
9 [Thurs]	Began a sowing wheat
10	Michealmas Day Old
13	Began to get Potatoes
15	Mr Chadwick Ordaind at Deanrow
20	Got done Getting Pottatoes

1788	November
5 [Wed]	Went to Mr Marslands B[ullock] Smithy had
	a dance
6	Began to get Turnips for Cows
15	Covered the Asparagus

Diary
p 63

24

Laid in the Cows

[1788]	**December**
2 [Tues]	Bramhall Court
20	Laid in the horses

1789	**January**
17 [Sat]	Sold Mr Fidler One Stack of hay

[1789]	**February**
13 [Fri]	Went to a dance at Mr Marslands of Bullock Smithy
20	Began a ploughing for oats Laid in the Colts
22	Set peas
27	Do Pottatoes

[1789]	**March**
20 [Fri]	Stockport Illuminated on his Majesty's recovery

1789	**March**
21	Begun sowing Oats

Diary p 64

[1789]	**April**
11 [Sat]	Sowd onions Lettices Carrots etc
14	Sowd Barly
17	Got done Sowing Oats
23	General thanksgiveings throug the Kingdom

[1789]	**May [April overwritten]**
11 [Mon]	Got done Setting Pottatoes
13	Went to play at Manchester
14	Set Kidney Beans Sow'd cucmber seed
15	Got done make summer work
16	Turnd cows into Grass

WOODFORD NEW HALL

GLOSSARY

The glossary explains the words in the diary which are printed in **bold**. They appear in alphabetical order according to the original spelling (except where the modern spelling is almost the same eg **MICHAELMAS** for **MICHEALMAS**). Within the glossary the same rule applies; words in the text in **bold**, as well as those marked "See", can be found in alphabetical order elsewhere in the glossary. The names of people appear under their surname. In some cases, where a family is concerned, the entry will appear as the name followed by "family", eg **BIRCH FAMILY**. By following the references within a particular topic more background information can be obtained, eg **COURT** covers a wide variety of courts, their business and their terminology. The bibliography contains all the books and manuscripts we have used.

ACCOMPTS
Brother William **(27 November 1783)** aged 12 and sister Mary **(2 February 1784)** aged 10 'begun accompts'. It is thought they were being taught to keep accounts (book keeping).

ACRE
A measure of land, thought to derive from the area of land a team of oxen could plough in one day. A statute acre is 4,840 square yards.

ACRE, CHESHIRE
The Cheshire acre was approximately two and a half times larger than the statute acre, being 10,240 square yards.

AFFEEROR, see COURT OFFICIALS

ALCOCK, MISS J
An Alcock family lived at Gatley Hill House and had strong nonconformist connections in the district. They were involved in cotton manufacturing. **(23 November 1785)**

ALE AND BEER
Ale was the older drink and was made from malted **barley**. It was mild and sweet but did not keep very long. Beer started to be made when hops were introduced from Flanders around the 16th century. These gave beer its characteristic bitter taste and improved its keeping quality. Hops were used in the ratio of one pound of hops to one **bushel** of **malt**. See BREWING BEER

ALE HOUSE
From the medieval period women had brewed ale for their families and employees. Some also brewed for sale. They used to hang a "bush" outside their houses to advertise their product. It is thought that this custom originated from the hanging up of the "besom" or bunch of broom used to stir the fermenting liquor at the **brewing** stage. It was impregnated with yeast and would start the beer working more

quickly. In Bramhall between 1780 and 1788 there were eight licens-
ed ale house keepers. Several are mentioned in the diary including
Ann Hough, whose family had been licensees from at least 1754. See
ALE SELLING, LICENCE; GLAVE, JOHN; and GOULDEN, JAMES

ALE SELLING LICENCE
There have been controls over the selling of ale since 1266. The
ale or beer was usually brewed at the alehouse and its quality and
price regulated by "ale tasters" or "conners" who were local
inspectors appointed by the **vestry** or **manor**. As early as 1286 one
Sineon of Bromale was presented for breaking the Assize of Ale and
was fined 12d. From 1552 all **ale house** keepers had to be licensed
by the local **justices of the peace**. In 1640 William Grosvenor of
Bramhall was presented at **Quarter Sessions** by John Massey and
William Huxley, petty **constables** of Bramhall, for selling ale
without a licence. Peter Pownall refers to John **Glave** receiving his
licence. **(11 September 1783)**. See RECOGNIZANCE ROLL

AMERCEMENT
A minor financial penalty imposed in a **manor court**.

APPEARANCE
The first Sunday that a newly-married couple were at home after
their wedding was known as "Showing-off Sunday". They were expected
to attend church wearing their wedding clothes and to hear the
wedding anthem "Thy wife shall be as a fruitful vine". On the way
to and from church the husband walked in front of his wife to show
who was master! We doubt whether the gentry observed the custom.
(15 June 1783)

ARDEN (ARDERNE)
The Ardernes of Harden Hall were owners of part of the manor of
Bredbury about 1672. Later Sir John Arderne purchased the rest on
the death of its owner William Davenport of Henbury. In 1761 John
Arden (he preferred this spelling of the family name) was High
Sheriff of Cheshire. The Arden family had a town house in Stockport
about the end of the 15th Century. This lovely timber-framed house
is now the National Westminster Bank in Underbank. **(6 January 1787)**

ASPARAGUS
This vegetable has been known in England since the 17th century and
probably before. It is considered a delicacy today. The plant can
be damaged by heavy frost so Peter **Pownall** covered his asparagus
beds with **straw** to protect them **(26 October 1782)**. He grew a wide
variety of **vegetables**. See MARKET GARDENING

BANKS, MR
Possibly Sir Joseph Banks (1743-1820), an explorer and naturalist.
He travelled extensively to collect specimens, including sailing
round the world with Captain Cook. He was the honorary director of
the Royal Botanic Gardens at Kew, and president of the Royal Society
in 1778. The Manchester Mercury, of 12 February 1788, announces a
course of twelve lectures on experimental philosophy to be given by
him in Manchester beginning on 24 March. **(24 March 1788)**

BARLEY

Barley is a hardy form of cereal which is mainly used to make **beer**, being **malted** first at a kiln. Arthur Young, writing in 1773, mentions the large quantity of barley grown for sale to the **malt** kilns of Manchester, and Thomas Wedge, in a report for the Board of Agriculture dated 1794, mentions barley and **oats**; and barley, oats and **turnips** being **rotated** as crops on the various sandy soils of Cheshire. Later less barley was grown and by 1836 only 3.6% of the arable land in Cheshire was used to grow barley compared with 31.4% used for **wheat** and 32.1% for oats. Peter Pownall took his barley to a mill kiln at **Dean Row** near Wilmslow. **(13 November 1782)**

BARLEY GROUND

Peter **Pownall rotated** his crops. He may be referring to the field name (there are two on the Bramhall tithe map but neither is on his farm) or, more likely, he may be following last year's crop of **barley** with **wheat**. **(13 November 1782)**

BARON COURT see COURT BARON

BAY MARE

A chestnut-coloured female **horse**. **(12 November 1784)**

BEANS see MARKET GARDENING and VEGETABLES

BEAR-BAITING

This was a popular sport with every class of society - even Queen Elizabeth I had her own bears. "Baits" provided an opportunity for gambling. The bears were taken by their handlers or "bear-wards" to **fairs** and **wakes**. The bear was tied to a stake and one or more dogs were set upon it. The results can be imagined. Another diarist, Edward Burgnall, wrote of a bear-ward at the Bunbury **Wakes** in 1628 who was "cruelly rent into Pieces by a Bear and soe died fearfully". He thought this was "God's judgment". Some bears were trained to "dance" to entertain the public. These bears were muzzled.

BEEHIVES

The best beehives or skeps were made of rye straw. To keep them waterproof caps of thatch were made and replaced every three to four months. From 1851 wooden hives were made with detachable wooden frames which enabled the collection of honey without killing the **bees**. Peter **Pownall** refers to thatching his beehives so he must have used straw ones. **(14 November 1782)**. See BEES, KEEPING.

Thatched beehive

BEER see ALE AND BEER

BEES, KEEPING

Honey, because of its sweetness, has been a valuable part of the human diet for thousands of years. The Bible has numerous references to wild honey and the ancient Greeks were known to have kept bees. The wild insects were encouraged to occupy simple hives made of basketwork or earthenware. In Britain before the middle of the 19th century bees were housed in skeps made from straw bound with willow and shaped rather like inverted waste paper baskets, with a slit some 15cm wide and 5cm deep at the bottom for the bees to enter. The skeps were placed on stone bases in wall recesses. The only way to collect the honey was to kill the bees inside. The owner usually selected the heaviest skeps (most honey) and the lightest (weakest colony) and, putting them into a pit, killed the bees by burning sulphur under them. The honey and beeswax were then available. The empty skeps were re-used to house new swarms of bees. (17 October 1782)

BENISON
Benison, or Bennison, is an old Bramhall name. The first reference we have found was in 1662 when William Bennison was in conflict with the **farmer** of the Bramhall **tithes**. In the early 1700s the Benisons farmed land near Bramhall **Mill** where they had a "watering place". In the court rolls (1716) they were instructed to put a foot **bridge** over the mill stream but to prevent carts from crossing. In 1742 a John Bennison was gamekeeper to William **Davenport**. In 1783 Peter **Pownall** was a witness to the will of Peter Benison, a weaver. His grandson, William Benison, is mentioned in the diary **(18 October 1783)**. Peter Pownall records the birth of two children to Mary Benison. **(8 November 1782 & 27 November 1783)**

BENISON'S PLACE
A Thomas Benison appears in the land tax assessment for Hillgate, Stockport in 1716. He was also a tenant at Bramhall. **(20 January 1786)**. See STOCKPORT CHAPEL

BIRCH FAMILY
The Birch family had early connections with the **Pownalls**. In 1580 Humphrey Pownall was witness to the will of John Birch, husbandman. In 1687 the Rev Eliezer Birch was pastor at **Dean Row Chapel**. Peter Pownall's mother, Alice (née Birch), was the second wife of Peter Pownall senior. They were married on 16 October 1759, at St **Mary's Church**, Stockport. Miss Birch, who died on 8 October 1782, was probably a close relative as her clothes were "divided out" by Peter Pownall's mother and his sister, Sarah. **(5 March 1783)**

BIRCH, MISS see BIRCH FAMILY

BIRCH WINE
This wine was made from the sap of mature birch trees, drawn in March when it is rising. A tube is inserted into the bark and the sap runs down it to be collected in a jug hanging below. About one gallon can be taken from a tree in two days. The hole must then be well plugged and a tree tapped only in alternate years to protect it. One recipe requires a gallon of sap, three pounds of sugar (or a quart of honey), citric acid in the form of lemons and oranges, and a pound of raisins. This produces a fine sweet wine. It is said to have been very popular in the 19th century with the Prince Consort. **(27 March 1784)**

BLACKSMITH AND FARRIER
Originally these were two separate crafts. The blacksmith was a worker in iron and heavy metals, the farrier shod horses and was also known as a "shoesmith". Since both required a forge, the separate crafts often became allied and were carried out by one man. The village **smith** undertook a wide range of tasks. He made and repaired a great variety of tools and wares from plough shares to saucepans, and provided many iron parts such as hinges for doors and gates. He also worked with the **wheelwright**. In his capacity as a farrier he gained much experience with horses and was often regarded both as a horse doctor and as an amateur vet for other domestic animals. Occasionally cattle, being driven the hundreds of miles to London, were also shod to protect their hooves. This has been offered as an explanation for the old name of a nearby village, **Bullock Smithy**.

BOONWORK
Labour service due by a tenant to his lord. In the 17th century boonwork in Bramhall leases included ploughing, **harrowing**, **mucking** and **shearing**. Later, in the 18th century, a payment of a few pence could be made in lieu.

BOWS see POTATOES, CULTIVATION OF

BRAMALL HALL
Home of the Davenport family from the 14th century until 1877. See MANOR

BRAMHALL COURT see COURT BARON

BRAMHALL GREEN
This was the site of the original village of Bramhall. It is the area by the east entrance to Bramall Hall around the present roundabout at the junction of Bramhall Lane South and Bridge Lane. There was a school (see SCHOOL, BRAMHALL), the Shoulder of Mutton Inn, a blacksmith, a tailor, a police constable, the **pinfold** and the **stocks**. At one time it was the "Towns Meadow" and may have been common land. **(11 January 1783)**. See GOULDEN,JAMES

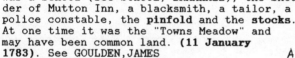

A

PUSH PLOUGH
IN USE.

BREAST PLOUGH or PUSH PLOUGH
This was a type of "man-plough" used for paring turf. The handle was held at chest (or breast) height to enable the implement to be pushed forwards. After paring the turf was burned and ploughed into the ground. An entry in the **court rolls** for 1719 states "We **amercy** Thomas Fawkner for digging up and burning soyle in the highway". A "Push Plough field" is shown on the Bramhall **tithe** map dated 1842.

31

BREWING BEER

There are three stages in brewing beer. First the **malt** is soaked in hot water to extract the sugars, "mashing". Then the liquor or wort is strained off and boiled with hops (modern beer has sugar added at this point). Finally it is strained again and cooled to a temperature of 60F (15C), when the yeast is added. The liquor is left to ferment for two to seven days. The resulting beer is drained off the yeast and put into casks, "racking". The washed or "swilled" malt grains were fed to the **pigs** as "pig swill" and the yeast could be used to make bread. We do not know whether yeast was dried to keep it for the next brew or whether the spores left within the brew tubs or the bush started the fermentation in medieval times. See ALE AND BEER and ALEHOUSE

BRIDGES, MAINTENANCE OF

The maintenance of some bridges on **highways** was the responsibility of the county but most public bridges were the responsibility of the **hundred** and the rate for their upkeep, although imposed by **Quarter Sessions**, was levied on the hundred. Local bridges had to be built and repaired by the inhabitants of the **township**, who were obliged to turn out and labour physically. See HIGHWAY, MAINTENANCE OF. In Bramhall in 1637 William Rowcrofte and Thomas Richardson undertook to repair a bridge on the payment of one penny by everyone. About 1680 a new bridge, known as **Woman's Croft Bridge**, was built.

BRIDGES, TYPES OF

There were several grades of bridges. The smallest was a footbridge for pedestrians only, the next was a riding bridge for horses, and the largest a cart bridge. An example of the last in Bramhall was Woman's Croft Bridge. There were many footbridges or **plats** all of which had to be kept in good repair for public use. The **court rolls** contain many references to bridges over streams and ditches: "We Paine the Occupants of Benissons ground to lay a Foot platt over the Milne dam betwixt the hemps clouh and the Pingott ... paine 3s 4d" in the summer court of 1716.

BRIDGE, WOMAN'S CROFT

This Bramhall bridge crossed the Ladybrook near to the junction of Bridge Lane and Valley Road, and was named after the croft divided by the present road (Woman's Croft). The original name of Bridge Lane was **Mill** Lane, and the bridge was also known as Mill Bridge. The old bridge was demolished about 1930, the road straightened and the new bridge constructed at an oblique angle to the stream. See Appendix 4

BROCKLEHURST FAMILY

The earliest reference we have found to the family is an Oliver Brocklehurst of Glossop in the early 16th century. His descendants lived at Gap House, Taxal for several generations. See Appendix 6b

BROCKLEHURST, JOHN (1754-1839)

John Brocklehurst married Sarah, Peter Pownall's sister, at St **Mary's Church** Stockport on 27 March 1783. She was his second wife (Sarah Massey of Rainow, his first wife, had died soon after the birth of their daughter Sarah in November 1781). John joined Acton

& Street, button manufacturers, in 1745. This firm expanded to
include silk throwing and subsequently, under his sons J & T Brocklehurst, became the largest silk cloth manufacturers in England.
John and Sarah lived at Pear Tree House, now Jordangate House,
Macclesfield.

BROCKLEHURST, JOHN (1788-1870)
Third child of John and Sarah Brocklehurst. From 1812, with his
brother Thomas, he was a silk manufacturer employing 8,000 workers.
He was also a partner in the family bank. In 1814 he married Mary
Coare, sister of his brother William's wife. In 1832 he became the
first Member of Parliament for the Borough of Macclesfield and held
the seat for 36 years.

BROCKLEHURST, MISS (?-1827)
Miss Sarah Brocklehurst was the daughter of the Rev William
Brocklehurst of Dean Row Chapel. **(8 May 1788)**

THE BROCKLEHURSTS RENOVATED SOME
OF THE POWNALL GREEN COTTAGES.

BROCKLEHURST, SARAH nee POWNALL (1762-1843)
Sarah was Peter Pownall's sister, three years his elder. On 27
March 1783 she became the second wife of John **Brocklehurst** of
Macclesfield and bore him three sons and a daughter: William **(20
February 1784)**, Mary **(4 August 1786)**, John (30 October 1788) and
Thomas (27 January 1791). Sarah's marriage, the dates and times of
birth of her first two children, their baptisms and **inoculations** are
recorded in her brother's diary. Three weeks before her marriage
she visited Manchester with her mother to buy **wedding clothes (5
March 1783)**. Almost three months after her wedding she "made her
appearance" as a married lady at **Dean Row Chapel**. Her first visit
home after her **lying-in** following William's birth was also noted **(4
May 1784)**. Sarah and her husband predeceased Peter Pownall. Sarah

was buried at Macclesfield. William died without issue within a year of his uncle's death, so John and Thomas inherited **Pownall Hall** with the rest of the property, which was gradually sold off. See MARRIED, SISTER SARAH

BROCKLEHURST, REV WILLIAM (1721-1786)
He was the minister of **Dean Row Chapel** from 1748 until his death on 3 September 1786, and introduced **Unitarian** doctrines and practices while he was there. He inherited Legh (Lee) Hall in Mottram St Andrew from his father William (1672-1754), a **chapman** who had bought the hall in 1751.

BROCKLEHURST, WILLIAM (1784-1859)
Sarah's first child, who became a solicitor and a manager of the family bank, and married Ann Coare of Islington in 1812. **(20 February 1784)**

B SMITHY see BULLOCK SMITHY

BULL-BAITING
The specially-trained bull was taken by its keeper to a roped enclosure and tied to a strong post with a rope, about 6 or 7 metres in length, through a ring in its nose. Then a dog, often a bulldog, was loosed and encouraged to attack the bull. The dog that bit and hung on to the bull's nose the longest was judged to have won. Much money was gambled on the results. Bull-baits were held at **Old Fold Farm**, Hazel Grove, up to the end of the last century.

BULLOCK
Originally a young bull or bull calf, now always a **castrated** bull.

BULLOCK, MARY nee POWNALL
She was Peter **Pownall's** cousin (daughter of Benjamin Pownall). Peter Pownall was acting on behalf of his father, who was an executor of the will of John Pownall (1775). This includes a legacy of £20 to be paid to Mary within a year of her father's death (1785). As Mary had married John Bullock in 1783 **"dowray"** seems inappropriate. **(31 March 1786)**. See Appendices 5 & 6

BULLOCK SMITHY
The old name for the village of Hazel Grove, changed in 1836 in an effort to improve its reputation. The original name may have come from Richard Bullock who had a smithy there in the 17th century, the nearby inn of that name or even the **blacksmith** shoeing bullocks. **(5 November 1788)**

BURRIID
?buried. Possibly Thomas Shacroft was killed when the sides of a **marl pit** he was digging collapsed on him. **(4 November 1782)**

BURY-ST-EDMUNDS
Martha **Davenport** was born in Hesset, Suffolk, and married at Bury St. Edmunds in 1767. Possibly this was a visit to relations. **(19 November 1782)**

BUSHEL see WEIGHTS AND MEASURES

BUTS see BUTTS

BUTTS
(1) Butt.   In this area the system of butts and reins was commonly
used on heavy or wet land. Looking similar to medieval ridge and
furrow but in straight lines, the butts were strips from 2-3 metres
wide drained on either side by furrows, which in turn drained into a
ditch at the edge of the field.   Peter **Pownall** refers to preparing
ground in this way for "next year's **potato** crop " **(12 November 1782)**
and to "drawing **summer work**" into butts in July or August.   Whether
this is the ploughing of fallow land for next year's **wheat** or the
ploughing of land cleared of a previous crop we cannot tell.   **(24
August 1784)**.
(2) Butt. An irregularly shaped piece of land in the **common** field
(3) Butts. Area used for archery practice. In 1639 the **constable** of
Bramhall was presented before the **manor court** for not repairing the
butts.   The name is thought to have come from the use of the end of
a barrel (butt) as the target.

CALVED
From .Christmas until May cows were kept in sheds or **shippons**.   It
was during this period that most calving took place.   Peter
Pownall's black cow had her first calf in January **(7 January 1783)**.
Calves for herd replacement were weaned at three weeks and fed on
whey, buttermilk and **oatmeal**. Young bull calves and others surplus
to requirements were frequently sold to butchers, to save the
expense of feeding them **(4 February 1784)**.   According to the
announcement of the sale of stock at **Pownall Hall** shortly after
Peter Pownall's death, he had been renowned for his "young dairy
cows, **heifers** [and] young cattle". These "were selected with great
care and judgement".   His "superior knowledge of cattle" was
"proverbial". See CATTLE and Appendix 5b

CANDLEMAS DAY see SAINTS' DAYS

CARPET
Carpets on the floor were still a luxury at this time and were
usually quite small.   The new English manufacturers in Axminster,
Kidderminster, Wilton, etc competed with the traditional imported
eastern carpets from Turkey, Persia and India.   Architects such as
Robert Adam designed carpets to match their highly decorated
ceilings.   Since Peter Pownall is getting a new carpet **Pownall Hall**
must have been well furnished **(22 March 1783)**.   The carpet was
bought only five days before the wedding of Sarah **Pownall** and John
Brocklehurst. We wonder whether the reception was held at the hall.

CARROTS
It is probable that Peter Pownall grew "field carrots" which were
used as **fodder** for cattle in winter and not for human consumption.
(4 December 1782)

CARTS
The two-wheeled cart was commonly used in Cheshire.   After 1770 the

four-wheeled wagon was used by many farmers because of the improvement in the condition of the **roads** due to the establishment of turnpike trusts. At the time of his death Peter **Pownall** owned several carts. See Appendix 5b

CART TAX
This tax applied to two-wheeled and, originally, springless open **carts** drawn by one horse, and was 10s a year. When used mainly for agricultural or trade purposes a reduced duty was charged. The words "a taxed cart" and the owners name and place of abode had to be written on the cart.

CASTRATED
Castration or gelding is the surgical removal of the sexual organs of a male animal. Colts are castrated at a year old to quieten their temperaments so that they can live and work with other horses without fighting. **(21 April 1783)**

CASUAL LABOURERS
Peter Pownall employed men and boys on a temporary basis, usually at harvest time, although occasionally they did weeding and mowing (hay making). From 1796-1812 he employed 5-11 casual labourers per year and recorded between 49 and 140 man days per season. The annual harvest period between 1782 and 1788 lasted approximately one calendar month. The same labourers were employed in successive years and, judging by the surnames, were often several members of the same family. For example no fewer than eight members of the Brown family are mentioned of whom one, John, was employed from 1796 to 1812. A John Brown also paid rent for a cottage. Casual labour was also provided by the Leah family, Thomas Leah senior working nearly as often as John Brown. There is no evidence of Peter Pownall employing casual Irish labourers. See LIVE and WAGES and Appendix 2

CATECHISM
Although the Anglican Catechism was not used by the **Unitarians** it appears that they may have used the shorter form, such as was used in Scotland, which had certain features removed that were considered objectionable. Presumably it was this shorter catechism that Mr **Brocklehurst** taught. **(15 May 1785)**

CATICHISING see CATECHISM

CATTLE
In the 18th century there were several different terms to distinguish cattle: bullock (a young bull), oxen (heavy beasts used for ploughing or drawing loads), steers (either bullocks for beef or draught oxen), and kine or kie (cows) **(15 October 1782)**. See HEIFER; STIRK, and CALVED.

CHAPMAN
This term applies to a man who bought and sold goods, such as a merchant, a trader or an itinerant pedlar. In the case of William **Brocklehurst** senior the first seems most likely.

CHEADLE HULME COURT
The **Court Baron** was held at the Horse and Jockey Inn on the site of what is now the Hesketh Arms. **(11 December 1782)**

CHEESE see CHEESEMAKING

CHEESEMAKING
The making of cheese was usually the job of the women on the farm, often the farmer's wife. As each farm had its own method cheese varied in texture and flavour. The local grass and plants fed to the cows, and the bacteria which impregnated the wooden utensils, also affected the cheese, hence the many varieties. Cheesemaking was mainly a summer occupation when the yield of milk was highest and on the Pownall farm began in April or May and finished in November or December. The yield from one or two successive milkings was poured into a vat and **rennet** added, and the mixture was left to curdle. The solid matter (the curds) was strained from the liquid (the whey), cut up and kneaded, and salt and sometimes colouring (like carrot juice) were added. The curds were then put into a cheese press and left until they were solid.

CHEESE, POWNALL
Cheese references in the diary are not comprehensive but analysis of the available data shows that in 1783, after the sale of an unspecified quantity of cheese at £2 10s per cwt (hundredweight), the **Pownalls** still had a further 19 cwt for sale **(31 January and 5 February 1783)**. Three years later cheese was only fetching £1 10s per cwt and sales were down to 15 cwt **(10 February 1786)**. There are no further references to cheese until 1807 when the Pownall family were purchasing it from John **Goulden** and Mr Dodge. We presume that as the profits from cheesemaking decreased so the dairy herd was reduced. Stella Davies notes that between 1801 and 1810 the price of cheese rose to £4 per cwt but the Pownalls did not restart production. See WEIGHTS AND MEASURES

CHEESE ROOMS
Cheese was often stored in a room above the cow house so that the rising warmth would help it to ripen.

CHEESE SELLING
In 1783 Peter **Pownall** sent cheese to Robert Haveyard, who may have been a cheese factor acting as an **agent (8 February 1783)**. The next year it was a Mr Priestnall who weighed the Pownall's cheese **(26 February 1784)**. But it was sent to market, possibly **Stockport (13 March 1784)**. We do not know the reason why. Many cheese factors were reputed to be less than honest, which may account for the change.

CHESHIRE ACRE see ACRE, CHESHIRE

CLOVER
Red clover was sown on its own or in combination with **rye** grass or other **trefoils** as pasture on land previously used for arable **(27 June 1785)**. Once the crop was mown the roots could be ploughed in to enrich the soil and prepare it for arable use again. **(8 November 1785)**. See ROTATED CROPS

COCK FIGHTS

Cock fights were held in cock-pits about six metres in diameter. The birds were specially trained and prepared. The comb was cut off, as were the tail, head and shoulder feathers to prevent them being seized by the opponent. The wing feathers were trimmed to dart-like points, the claws were sharpened and steel spurs were fitted. As many as 200 people assembled to watch the fights and gamble on the results. Fights lasted up to 15 minutes until one of the birds was either killed or bled to death. Cock fighting, although illegal since 1849, was reported as occurring in Hazel Grove until the beginning of the present century.

COLT

A young male horse up to the age of 4 or 5 years. (10 October 1782)

COMMON See WASTE

COMMON ARABLE LAND OR OPEN FIELD

It seems likely that Bramhall had areas of arable land that were held in common and were divided into strips. Evidence found so far is sparse. Field names include a "Town Meadow" and "One Dole" (a selion or strip). The position of some fields with like names on the tithe map of 1842 also suggests that they were originally part of one common field. For example in northwest Bramhall there are seven fields close together that have "Shotsall" as part of their names. "Infield and Outfield" may have been practised, when the better-quality land was regularly used for arable (infield) and at times of famine or population pressure the second-rate land (outfield) was brought into cultivation. Each villager held a number of scattered strips within the open field. Later these holdings were rationalised and **inclosed**. A few strips escaped and are visible on the **tithe** map on Patch Lane and near Birch Hall. These should not be confused with the **mossrooms**.

COMMONER

One who had common rights with his neighbours. In Bramhall he had **common of pasture** and **common of turbary** but there were restrictions on the use of wood. Some tenants were allowed hay bote (the right to take wood to repair fences), housebote (wood to repair buildings) and fire bote (wood for burning). Usually timber or underwood was allowed for boarding ditches. Tenants were encouraged to take **marl** to improve their land. In 1654 a householder in Woodford was accused of taking "ridging clods upon the waste of Bramhall".

COMMON LAND

This could be arable, meadow, pasture or **waste** land, such as parts of the **moors**, and even road side verges which were subject to some form of common use and regulation by the manorial community. See MOORLOOKER and MOSS ROOM

COMMON OF PASTURE

This was the right of householders in a manor to graze their livestock on the **common land** or **waste**. In August 1654 the Bramhall **manor court** established that the sides of a "Lane or highway...belongeth for Comon of Pasture". The number of cattle using the common was stinted (limited) according to the size of land holding to prevent over-grazing. In 1716 John Hadfield was presented for "overchargeing Snibbs Moore in with callfes". Three years later William Holt was accused of the same on Kitts **Moor**.

CONSTABLE, HEAD OR HIGH

Two head constables were appointed for each Cheshire **Hundred**. They saw that each **township** had a petty **constable** and with the local JPs supervised him in his duties. They were responsible for the rates and taxes that were collected, drew up a list of freeholders liable for jury service and attended **quarter sessions**. By the 19th century their responsibilities had decreased and the office was abolished in 1870.

CONSTABLE LAY see CONSTABLE, PETTY and LAY OR LAY

CONSTABLE, PETTY

Originally the constable was appointed by the **manor court** but by 1662 he was supervised and sworn in by the local JP. Constables were elected to preserve the peace but they should not be confused with the modern policeman. Their duties were many and onerous including:

    preventing affrays and riots
    arresting and keeping prisoners under guard pending trial
    ensuring provision and maintenance of local means of punishment
        such as **stocks**, scolds bridle or whipping posts
    settlement or removal of **strangers** and beggars
    seeing to the selection and training of local **militia** and
        maintenance of the town's weapons
    stopping cursing and swearing, unlawful games or drinking and
        eating of meat during fast days
    supervising strolling players and minstrels
    inspecting **ale houses** and control of **weights and measures**

They were responsible for carrying out the sentences of the JPs, whipping rogues and vagabonds, ducking scolds, etc. They were also responsible for collecting local and national taxes and **distraining** the goods of those who failed to pay. At first the petty constable could claim payment only for his expenses, but after 1662 he could also charge for time spent on duty. Early records show only one petty constable for the five **townships** of Bramhall, Handforth-cum-Bosden, Norbury, Offerton and Torkington. He was paid by the **overseers of the poor** for each township, from money collected as a constable **lay** or tax. Peter **Pownall** paid Joseph Clarke 8s 2d as a constable lay **(19 October 1782)**. In 1831 three of the Stockport JPs at Knutsford Quarter Sessions recommended an increase in the number of petty constables and a separate one was appointed for each township. The Bramhall constable received a salary of £18 per year, paid quarterly. The constables had to keep accounts which were handed to the overseers for inclusion in their own accounts. The office was unpopular and often second-rate men performed the duties on behalf of others, for payment.

CORN

In America "corn" usually means maize, corn on the cob or sweet corn. In Britain the word "corn" is usually applied to the main

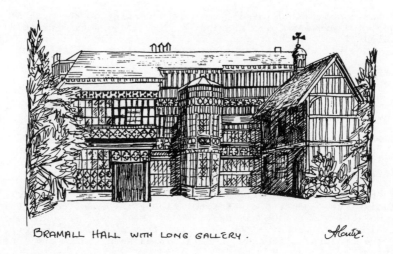

BRAMALL HALL WITH LONG GALLERY.

cereal crop of an area, whether it be **oats**, **barley** or **wheat**. It is not clear exactly which grain Peter **Pownall** means by "corn" as he writes of all of these. **(12 October 1782)**

COURSING see HARE COURSING

COURT BARON
Bramhall manor court was called the baron court. It was held by the steward of the lord of the manor and all the lord's tenants - free, villein or serf - had to attend or pay an **amercement**: "We present all persons who owe suit and service to ... pay 4d a piece ... for non-appearance at every Court except a lawful cause to be showed to the contrary" (Court Rolls of Bramhall, Midsummer 1721). The obligation to attend court appeared in Bramhall leases, for example Richard Brocke, 26 August 1673, had to pay **suit and service**.

COURT, BRAMHALL see COURT BARON

COURT, BUSINESS OF THE
Bramhall **Court Rolls** include presentments for:
    neglect of property - houses, outbuildings, fences and gates
    failure to perform services such as **boon work**, **highway main-
       tenance**, etc
    failure to use the lord's **mill**
    encroachment on **waste**, **common**, **forest** or a neighbour's land
    poaching
    allowing stock to stray
    harbouring **strangers** for **settlements**
Other matters included land transfers with **heriots** and **entry fines**, settling of disputes and debts, and upkeep and marking of manor boundaries.

COURT EYRE
The name is thought to come from the Latin "itinere" (on a journey).
From 1166 the King sent his own justices to tour the country and sit
in court to hear matters relating to the crown and administration of
each county. However Cheshire was different from the rest of
England and there is no evidence to show that a general eyre was
held in the county. Each Cheshire **hundred** had an eyre which was a
court of general criminal jurisdiction. Some of the offences
recorded in the Macclesfield Eyre Rolls in 1286 were: murder,
stealing, selling false measure or substandard produce, such as
ale, bread and meat. Some cases related to the **forest** law: hunting,
poaching or killing the earl's deer (venison), damage to the forest
by allowing animals to stray or overgraze, cutting the trees or
undergrowth (vert) and enclosing pieces of the forest (assarting).

COURT LEET
In Stockport the equivalent of the **manor court**. See FAIR, STOCKPORT

COURT OFFICIALS AND THEIR DUTIES

Affeeror	assessed the amount of the fines or penalty to be paid.
Alefounder	tested the quality of **ale and beer** sold within the manor. Also known as "aleconner" and "aletaster".
Burleyman	supervised the fences and collected straying animals.
Moorlooker	supervised the **commoners'** use of the land, its drainage and boundaries. There were four appointed in Bramhall, one for each of the four **moors** – Bramhall, Doghill, Kitts and Snibs.
Pinder	worked with the burleyman. He was in charge of the **pinfold** where straying animals were penned until the owner claimed them and paid a fine for their release.
Steward	was a man of standing, appointed by the lord to administer the manor and the court.
Weirlooker	in Bramhall supervised the weir and the leat and ordered the householders to maintain them.

COURT OF PIE POWDER
The name is thought to be a corruption of the French term "pieds
poudres" meaning dusty feet (which those who travelled the roads
would have) or the old French "pied puldreaux" meaning a pedlar.
The court was held in a building called the "tollbooth" or a nearby
tavern and took precedence during the **fair** or **market** over other
local courts. Both officers and merchants helped to dispense
justice, settle disputes between traders and keep order. Penalties
were swift – fines, floggings at the whipping post, or a period in
the pillory or **stocks** in the centre of the market-place.

COURT ROLLS
Records of the meeting of courts were known as court rolls. A roll
was a document consisting of one or more single sheets originally
attached end-to-end and stored by rolling. The records of the **Baron
Court** of Bramhall were written on separate sheets of parchment or
paper. These rolls, dating from 1716-1732, are deposited at the
Cheshire County Record Office (DDA/1533/1). The extracts for
1632-1657 are in W H Clemensha's article **"New Court of Bramhall"**

published by the Chetham Society, vol 80, 1921.   The original court
book cannot be traced.   No court records for the **Cheadle Hulme** court
have been found so far.

COURT ROLLS; SOME COMMONLY USED WORDS

Affeer	to fix the sum, at court, of a fine or amercement
Amerce	to fine - literally to be at the mercy of another as to the amount of a fine
Appraise	to fix a price or value, also of a fine
Assess	to fix the amount of tax or fine to be paid
Causey	causeway, a raised or paved way across low-lying wet land
Certificate	to excuse the manor from supporting **strangers** when they needed **relief**
Cleanse	of a ditch, to dig out so that water can flow
Cote keeper	owner of a cot or cottage
Croft	a small piece of enclosed arable land sometimes attached to a cottage
Ditch	verb - to dig out or scour a **ditch**
Enclosure	see **inclosure**
Essoign	legally excuse from a fine
Fine	(1) a payment or levy, eg an **entry fine** (2) a penalty
Fold	enclosure for domestic animals
Footwaye	footpath, paved or gravelled
Hayment	possibly a fence or fenced area of land
Heriot	at manor court, a payment made by heirs of a tenant on his death
Housing	a house, sometimes including, or being, out-buildings
Inclosure	(1) legal : a piece of manorial land enclosed with a fence or hedge for the use of a tenant; in Bramhall, usually with the agreement of the lord, who charged rent for it (2) illegal : inclosure of manorial land without such agreement
Incroachment	the enclosure of part of the **common** or another's land
Inmate	a sub-tenant, possibly a relation, a friend or a **stranger**
Intack	see **inclosure**
Intake	see **inclosure**
Lodger	may be a **stranger**
Meares)	in Bramhall, stones marking the boundary of the
Meres)	manor or fields
Mercy	amerce
Mill ditch	see **mill leat**
Millsoke	obligation of tenants to use the lord's **mill**
Moor	in Bramhall one of four areas of unenclosed waste
Moss	boggy land : in Bramhall, a peat bog. Synonymous with **moor**
Mossroom	see below
Mulcture	a fine for an offence
Multure	a toll paid to the miller for grinding **corn**
Over charging	putting more animals to graze on the **common land** or

	waste than allowed. See COMMOM OF PASTURE
Pain(e)	to punish; also peine
Privileges	on the **moor**, the right to graze stock, dig for peat, etc
Stranger	one who is living in the manor without a **settlement** or **certificate**.

CRIPS, MISSES
The only reference we can find is to Thomas Cripps, Rector of Cheadle, 1775-1794. He was assisted by Francis Cripps. It is possible that the ladies who visited Peter Pownall were related to one of these. **(17 March 1785)**

CROSS see CROSS PLOUGHING

CROSS PLOUGHING
The ground on which **barley** was grown was prepared by ploughing three times. The first time was in November; the second, in either March or April according to the weather, was followed by **harrowing**; and the third time preceded the **sowing** towards the end of April. **(12 April 1783)**

DAVENPORT, MR & MRS
William Davenport (1745-1829) was the 16th of the Davenport line and the 10th named William. The family had held the manor of Bramhall from about 1370 when John Davenport of Wheltrough married Alice de Bromale. William's beautiful wife, Martha, was the daughter of the Rev John le Tourcey, rector of Hesset in Suffolk. Sadly she bore William no children but seems to have agreed to the adoption of his two natural daughters, Anne and Maria. The girls were brought up at **Bramall Hall** and eventually Maria, who married Salusbury Pryce **Humphreys**, inherited the manor. Martha Davenport died on Christmas Day, 1810 and was the first person to be interred in the vault in Bramall Hall Chapel. William Davenport was also buried there and Peter **Pownall** was among the chief mourners. (In 1877, on the sale of the hall, all those buried in the chapel were re-interred at Cheadle Hulme graveyard).

DEAN ROW CHAPEL
This is said to be one of the oldest non-conformist places of worship in Macclesfield **Hundred**. Although the present building is thought to date from 1693, it is recorded that in 1672 one Robert **Birch** received a licence to preach and teach as an independent teacher in the Wilmslow area. The Rev Eliezer **Birch** was the first appointed pastor in 1687. During the 1850s the chapel, by then **Unitarian**, was restored and the graveyard enlarged. Peter **Pownall** and his brothers and sisters were all baptised here. See BROCKLE-HURST, REV WILLIAM

DEAN ROW CHAPEL; PEW RENTS
To raise money for a chapel it was customary to charge a pew rent which entitled a family to occupy the same pew every week. Peter **Pownall** paid this twice a year. He also paid subscriptions to the chapel of £1 1s 0d per quarter.

DEAN ROW CHAPEL.

DEAN ROW MALT KILN
Peter **Pownall** used a kiln at Dean Row for **malting** his **barley**. **(8 March 1783)**

DEATHS
The diary records the deaths of 27 acquaintances or relatives of Peter **Pownall**. Of three accidental deaths, two people were killed by horses **(8 October 1782 & 6 July 1787)** and one **"burriid"** **(4 November 1782)**. Two others are described as being "ill". The dangers of having babies during this period are emphasised by his reference to two ladies dying "of childbed" **(28 December 1784 & 5 December 1785)**. One friend was reported as burying his youngest son **(20 September 1785)**. The rest of those reported dying appear to be adults including one old lady who was aged 89 years **(23 January 1783)**.

DEPUTY LORD LIEUTENANTS see MILITIA

DESENTING MINISTER see DISSENTER

DIRT FAIR see MANCHESTER FAIRS

DISSENTER
One who refused to accept the doctrines of the established church and its ways of worship. **(23 November 1785)**

DISSENTERS' MEETING HOUSES
Under the 1689 Act the meeting places of dissenters had to be registered either with the bishop or with the **JPs**. Recorded for Bramhall were the houses of Thomas Taylor (9 January 1704/5) and Hugh **Worthington** (18 April 1710), Cheshire County Record Office, QDR MF 96/6.

DISTRAIN
To seize a person's goods to settle a debt or unpaid fine.

DITCHES
Ditches were necessary to drain boggy land and to collect water to irrigate dry areas. They needed to be cleared regularly and many inhabitants in Bramhall were presented at the **manor court** for not "ditching" their ditches. See MOORLOOKER and HIGHWAY MAINTENANCE.

DOCKED
Docking is cutting off all or part of an animal's tail. The reason for this is uncertain. It may have been for hygienic purposes or merely appearance. Docking was often done by a **blacksmith**. **(14 October 1783)**

DOOLY, JAMES see FARMWORKERS.

DOWRAY
John **Pownall** who died in 1775 had instructed in his will that his niece Mary **Bullock** (nee Pownall) be paid £20 within one year of the death of her father Benjamin, if she had reached the age of twenty-one. Benjamin died on 1 November 1785, so Peter **Pownall** is acting as executor in place of his father **(31 March 1786)**. See Appendix 5g

DUNGED see MUCKING

DYSON, MISS
Jane Dyson was the daughter of Alderman Joseph Dyson of Chester whose wife was the daughter of Smith Kelsall Esq of Bradshaw Hall, Cheadle. Jane married the Rev Charles **Prescot**, BD (Cantab), at Trinity Church, Chester on 18 June 1784. She died aged 56 on 26 March 1821, and was buried in the chancel of Stockport Parish Church, **St Mary's**. **(25 May 1784)**

EDDISH
Used to describe the second crop of grass cut from a field after the hay harvest. In the diary Peter **Pownall** could be using it as a temporary field name. **(20 September 1786)**

ELEVEN MONTHS see FARM WORKERS

EMERCY see COURT ROLLS, SOME COMMONLY USED WORDS - Amerce.

ENCLOSE see INCLOSED

ENTRY FINE
A money payment made to the lord of the **manor** by a new tenant on entering his tenancy. See HERIOT

ESTATES
The will of Peter **Pownall** dated 27 April 1857 shows that his lands were widely distributed. Not only did he own land in Bramhall (26 fields are shown on the 1841 Tithe map) but also in Mottram St Andrew, Cheadle Bulkley, Cheadle Moseley, Stockport, Handforth-cum-Bosden (**Old Fold Farm**), Hazel Grove and Marple. **(14 January 1783)**. See Appendix 5c, Peter Pownall's will.

EWE
A mature female sheep. **(13 December 1782)**

FAIRING
Literally a fairing is a gift given at or bought from a **fair**. **(18 October 1783)**. See HIRING FAIRS

FAIR, ALTRINCHAM
In 1290 Altrincham was granted a charter to hold a weekly market and an annual fair. **(22 November 1782)**. See FAIRS

FAIR, BARNABY
This fair was held at Macclesfield in June, near to the feast day of St Barnabas. **(23 June 1783)**. See FAIRS and SAINTS' DAYS

FAIRS
The word fair is thought to come from the Latin feria - a holiday. Fairs developed from markets where traders met to exchange their surplus goods. While markets were usually held on the same day each week, fairs were larger markets held once or twice a year. They often specialised in certain products (Stockport in cattle and cheese) and attracted traders from a distance. Naturally such gatherings were an excuse for merrymaking. **Ale houses** were open all day, food such as hot pies and gingerbread was sold, and there was much entertainment, from jugglers, tumblers and shooting matches, to **bear baiting**, tooth drawing, wrestling and even the whipping post. Small wonder that such occasions, lasting up to a week, led to riotous behaviour. They were not popular with all the townsfolk and attempts were made to shorten or ban them.

FAIRS, MANCHESTER
Three fairs were held in Manchester each year, Knott Mill, Whit Monday and Acres. A fourth, Dirt Fair, was held in Salford in the middle of November, This was primarily for the sale of **horses**, "horned cattle" and **pigs**, which may have given rise to its name. It was accompanied by sideshows and the other entertainments associated with **fairs**. **(18 November 1782)**

FAIRS, OFFICIALS
The organising and running of markets and fairs was the responsibility of officers appointed at the court of the lord who

held the charter. The steward was in charge and presided at the **Court of Pie Powder.** The market lookers worked under his supervision and their duties included checking the quality of the goods offered for sale and the accuracy of the **weights and measures** used. They also assessed the taxes and collected the tolls. Due to a shortage of goods for sale they had to prevent forestalling (that is selling goods before the market opening bell was rung) and engrossing (buying up large quantities) for regrating (resale).

FAIR, STOCKPORT
On 6 September 1260 the Lord Edward (eldest son of King Henry III, who had granted him the lordship of Cheshire without the title of earl) granted Sir Robert de Stokeport a charter to hold a weekly **market** and an annual **fair** in Stockport. This does not mean that no fair had been held before, but entitled Sir Robert to the tolls collected there. The fair began on St Wilfrid's day, originally 12 October. The adoption of the **new calendar** in 1752 changed the date to 23 October **(23 October 1782)**. The fair lasted eight days. In May 1633 Charles I granted Edward **Warren**, the then lord of the manor, two extra fairs, 20-21 April and 10-11 July, both with courts of **Pie Powder.** Peter **Pownall** noted the former **(1 May 1787)** as "new calendar". The latter was later discontinued. Around 1784 another charter established two fairs in March. **(3 and 25 March 1784)** In the 19th century the Stockport Fair opened with a procession of constables and other officers of the **Court Leet** from the manor house to the church, returning through the market place to the Warren Bulkley Arms Hotel "where an ample dinner was provided for the occasion".

FAIRS; STOCKPORT TOLLS
The grant to Sir Robert de Stokeport to hold a fair, gave him a new source of income which passed to each subsequent lord of the manor. He could levy tolls on all who entered the town, apart from burgesses of the borough, and on all goods sold - for example 4d for the sale of a horse and 2d for an ox. Whilst five sheep were charged at 1d the wool from their backs carried a toll of 4d. There was a charge for "standings" (stalls etc) and on goods sold from them. In 1779/80 the tolls collected on cheese alone amounted to £28 19s 6d.

FALLOWING
This is ploughing of land to make it ready for later sowing or to destroy weeds. Peter Pownall usually began fallowing in middle or late November and took anything from one week to more than a month to complete it. Availability of labourers and weather conditions probably account for the variation in the time taken. **(25 November 1782)**

FALLOW LAND
Land which is ploughed and **harrowed** but not seeded with a crop, to allow it to "rest" for a year or more. Stock was often grazed on such land to fertilize it. In Cheshire, from the 16th century, some fallow land was sown with grass seed and used as pasture for several years. See ROTATED CROPS

FALLOWS FAMILY

There are references to a Lawrence Fallows and his daughter, Elizabeth, in Bramhall as early as 1584. In 1604 Robert Fallows, a **blacksmith**, was a witness to Humphrey **Pownall's** will. In the early 18th century the family farmed near Doghill **Moor**. Phillip Fallows was presumably no longer young when he married **(7 August 1783)** and sadly his wife died in childbed the next year **(28 December 1784)**. In 1783 Thomas Fallows was chosen as **constable (21 October 1783)**. Richard Fallows was **overseer of the highways (13 October 1784)** and his goods sold, possibly **distrained. (12 June 1787)** In 1820 a John Fallows was landlord of the Anchor Inn on the Bramhall side of Hazel Grove. Samuel Fallows was a tenant of Salusbury Pryce **Humphreys**; he farmed near **Bramall Hall** and was hanged for murder in 1823. A John Fallows farmed at Grange Farm, Bramhall in the 1890s and was a member of Bramhall Parish Council.

FARMER

Originally this was a person who held an official position or a tract of land in return for the payment of a fixed sum of money known as a "farm" (Latin firma, a firm or fixed payment). In Stockport the right to collect **tithes** was farmed. In 1662 the Bramhall farmers were Nathaniel and Ann Tudway. William **Bennison** accused them of false dealing with the cattle with which he had paid his tithe. The case was heard before the Consistory Court at Chester (the Bishop's court). An earlier tithe farmer was a Peter Davenport.

FARM WORKERS

The **Pownall family** had live-in workers or servants, usually two female and three male. The men were farm labourers and probably at least one girl worked in the dairy. As was customary to prevent those who came from other **townships** claiming **settlement** (by being resident and employed for one year) Peter Pownall's workers were employed for "one year but a week" **(3 January 1785)**. Some may have been hired at **hiring fairs (18 October 1783)**. Occasionally families seem to be engaged; in 1807 Betty, Sarah and James Waters were employed. By the end of the 18th century live-in workers were generally young men and girls. The older workers lived with their families in cottages owned by the farmer; some were rent free but the **Pownall cottages** seem to have been let at 2s per week. See WAGES

FILIATION

Although the birth of illegitimate children during the 18th century caused little moral consternation, they were a charge on their mother's **township**. As the **overseers of the poor** wished to avoid this expense a pregnant unmarried woman was encouraged to declare the name of her child's father. If she refused the overseer could instruct the midwife to withhold assistance at the birth until the woman did confess. Then the two **JPs** issued a filiation order which compelled the father to pay towards the baby's birth and upkeep. If he failed to do so he could be put into gaol until he complied.

FLOUR

The accounts show that Peter Pownall sold flour to friends and neighbours. Quantities varied from £1 6s 0d worth to Peter Brown on 9 December 1806 to 3 loads at 50s a load to Mr William Davenport on 9 October 1809. There is only one mention of payment for grinding wheat, £1 16s 0d to "James Jarvis for Mr Pickles" on 13 January 1807. Those who lived on the manor were expected to use the lord's mill.

FLOWER see FLOUR

FOAL
A young horse of either sex, a colt or a filly. **(16 May 1787).** See HORSES

FODDER
Originally dried **hay** or **straw** used to feed **horses** and cattle which were housed in outbuildings during the winter **(9 and 26 November 1782).** By the end of the 18th century new crops like **turnips** were being used by progressive farmers like Peter **Pownall.** **(25 April 1787)**

FODDER, GREEN see WINTER FEED

FOREST
Possibly from the Latin "foris", land outside the common law and subject to forest law. A forest was not necessarily densely wooded. **Macclesfield forest** included moorland areas as well as wooded slopes.

FOREST, CHESHIRE
There were four forests in the medieval county of Chester: Wirral in the west, Delamere and Mondrum in the centre and Macclesfield in the east.

FOREST EYRE
This was a forest court introduced to Cheshire by the Black Prince as a means of raising revenue from fines. His justices visited Macclesfield in 1347 and 1357. At the second eyre the fines were very heavy. He also ordered the foresters to hold swainmote courts every three weeks to superintend the use of the forest, collect the dues and impose fines. See COURT ROLLS, SOME COMMONLY USED WORDS

FOREST, MACCLESFIELD
An early written reference to Macclesfield forest is a charter of Hugh II, Earl of Chester, about the middle of the 12th century when Richard Davenport was appointed Supreme Forester. The forests in Cheshire belonged to the Earl of Chester, not the King. They were subject to forest law which was administered by hereditary chief foresters. From 1684 Macclesfield forest was an administrative area only.

FOREST OF MACCLESFIELD; DAVENPORT CONNECTIONS
For generations members of the Davenport family were hereditary master serjeants of the peace of the Macclesfield Hundred. It is said that this empowered them to execute robbers captured in the forest. The John **Davenport** who married Alice, the last Bromale

(Bramhall) heiress around 1370, bore the family crest; this was "a felon's head couped proper, around the neck a halter or", ie a robber's head cut off, in natural colour, with a gold halter around the neck. This is the reason for the nickname of the Davenport Arms public house in Woodford, which is the Thief's Neck. Models of the crest can be seen at **Bramall Hall**.

FORTUNE see HULME FAMILY and Appendix 6a

GAME DUTY
Between 1784 and 1807 all persons, including manorial gamekeepers, who were qualified to kill or sell game had to register with the clerk of the peace and obtain a certificate in return for the fee.

GAME LICENCE
Game was defined as "bird" or "ground" and a licence was necessary for hunting. Three different licences were issued: red for a whole year, blue for November to July and green for August to October. Until 1880 no licence was required for hunting **rabbits** and **hares** although there was a closed season for hares from March to July inclusive. **(11 August 1786)**

GEESE
For hundreds of years geese have been useful members of the poultry yard being very hardy, long-lived and easy to keep. After foraging for food on the **waste** or **common land** by day, the flock would be brought home each evening to roost near the house where their loud cackling would act as a warning if they were disturbed by intruders. Each goose could lay up to 100 eggs a year and roast goose was traditional fare at **Michaelmas** and Christmas. The cooked bird yields a rich supply of goose grease, a fat which never hardens. This was used as a lubricant for machinery, to prevent metal from rusting and to waterproof leather, especially boots. The grease was added to wood ashes to make lye, a primitive soap. Within living memory goose grease was rubbed on to the chests of young children before they were sewn into flannel bodices for the whole winter, supposedly to protect them from illness! Peter **Pownall** noted plucking his geese. The soft under-feathers would have been used to fill mattresses, pillows and cushions. After the harvest had been gathered in the geese were turned onto the stubble with the other poultry to feed on the fallen grain. Some stubble geese were killed and eaten on **Michaelmas** Day. In the 17th and 18th centuries the **Davenport** tenants paid part of their rent in livestock, geese appear regularly in **inventories** and leases. Ralph Cooper in 1669 agreed to give one stubble goose (valued at one shilling) every September as part of his rent. **(4 August 1784)**

GEESE, SET
To "set" means to sit on eggs to hatch them. A goose will sit if well and regularly fed but often large hens were used instead. **(15 March 1783)**

GLAVE, JOHN
John Glave (sometimes Gleave) was the publican of the Lamb Inn from before 1767. This stood on Woodford Road opposite the Baptist Chapel

built in 1856. In 1783 the annual meeting for collecting **tithes** was held at this inn. The Lamb closed towards the end of the 19th century, and is now a private house. **(22 January 1783)**

GOULDEN or GOLDEN FAMILY
There are many references to Gouldens in Bramhall. The earliest we found was a Richard Golden connected with a transfer of land to John Davenport in 1445. A family of this name had a farm in 1716, probably near Yew Tree Road, Bramhall.

GOULDEN, JAMES
A James Goulden appears on **Recognizance Rolls** as an **ale house** keeper from 1768, we believe of the "Leg of Mutton" which stood on **Bramhall Green**. He also had a smithy there. The meeting to pay **lays** was probably held at his ale house **(25 December 1782)**. Peter Pownall paid him a bill for **"shewing"** **(15 September 1786)**. James Goulden died aged 61 in 1799 and his wife Sarah ten years later.

GOULDEN, JOHN
John Goulden rented property from Peter **Pownall** in 1807-8 for which he paid £40 twice a year (Accounts 6 January & 15 May 1807). Another entry shows a John Goulden who was employed as a **casual labourer** for harvest in 1798.

GOULDEN, THOMAS
Thomas Goulden was one of Peter **Pownall's** tenants. He may have been the Thomas Goulden who died on 7 February 1803 aged only 38 years. **(31 December 1784)**

GOULDEN, WILLIAM
William Goulden may have been the black sheep of the family. In 1822 he was arrested in connection with stealing linen from **Bramall Hall** and the following year he broke into the house of John Heginbotham off Bramhall Moor Lane. In July 1826 he was sentenced at Chester to 12 years hard labour for an assault on a ten year old girl in Bramhall woods.

GRAND FESTIVAL OF MUSICK
This was the Manchester Music Festival which took place from 21-23 September 1785. Devoted mainly to Handel's music, it included his "Samson" oratorio, sacred music and "Messiah". On two evenings there were concerts of miscellaneous items. Admission was by ticket only (one and a half guineas for the five performances) and servants were not allowed to "secure" the unreserved seats for their masters or mistresses. The ladies were requested to wear **hats** without feathers and only "small **hoops**". We do not know whether Peter **Pownall** attended the concerts. **(21 September 1785)**

GRIMSHAW, ROBERT
In 1791 a Robert Grimshaw of Gorton House, Gorton opened a weaving mill equipped with thirty Cartwright power looms at Knott Mill, Manchester. This early use of steam-powered looms was bitterly opposed by the hand loom weavers and within weeks the mill was set on fire and destroyed. This may be the Robert Grimshaw of the diary. **(14 January & 3 May 1788)**

HALLWORTH FAMILY

The Hallworth family appears in the **court rolls** of Bramhall as early as 1726. William and John, the sons of John Hallworth Snr, both served as **surveyors of the Highway**, William in 1782 when Peter **Pownall** paid him a **lay** of £1 12s 9d **(14 October 1782)**. Two years later John served with Richard Phallows **(Fallows)**. Peter Pownall reports the burning of a Mr Hallworth's warehouse **(18 January 1783)**. See LAY

HANGED

We have been unable to identify Pharoah and Phillis but there are no members of the family or staff with these names! **(18 October 1782)**

DATE
STONE

HARDY'S FARM   c 1900

HARDY FAMILY

For several generations the Hardy family lived at Hardy Farm on Ack Lane East. Hardy leases from the **Davenports** date from at least 1697. The house, with its date stone of 1745, is still standing (1988) but it seems likely that the date refers to house renovation rather than building. Like other ancient farmhouses in the area the building was probably timber framed originally. Between 1716 and 1732 Joshua Hardy frequently appeared as assessor at the Bramhall Baron **Court** and in 1728 was a burleyman. The **Pownall** and Hardy families seem to have been connected both socially and by trade. Peter Pownall Snr. (1707-91) and Robert Hardy (1722-1816) were both trustees of Jonathan Robinson's **school**. In January 1785 they exchanged **moss rooms** on Kitts Moss. The families visited each other to drink **tea** and to dine **(14 February 1788)**. Peter Pownall bought cattle and beef from a Mr Hardy (Accounts 1807-8), John Hardy buying

meal in return. There is also evidence that Peter Pownall lent
money to Robert Hardy (Accounts 1805), a common practice when
banking was still in its infancy. A Mr Hardy collected Peter
Pownall's taxes in 1807, possibly while performing the office of
overseer or **constable**. In 1822-3 a tragedy overtook the Hardy
family when father Robert and his three young sons aged 20, 18 and
16 all died within six months. See Appendix 6c & COURT OFFICIALS etc

HARE

The common hare (lepus timidus) is similar to a rabbit but has
larger ears and longer hind legs. Hares breed in March when they be-
have in a very lively manner. This has given rise to such sayings
as "mad as a March hare" and "hare-brained". The buck (male) is
nicknamed Jack Hare. Hares were caught for the table. See HARE,
JUGGED

WOODFORD OLD HALL.

HARE COURSING

Hare coursing is an ancient sport, known to the Greeks and Romans
but forbidden in England by the forest laws during the middle ages.
During the Stuart period it was the sport of gentlemen, who rode on
horseback while the lower orders followed on foot, with packs of
hounds known as a "cry". Later fox hunting took over as the
gentleman's sport but hare coursing is still practised today (eg
Waterloo Cup). Peter **Pownall** and his father often went hare
coursing with their friends in late autumn or in winter **(5 November**

1782). They coursed at Lostock, Styal, Mottram, Altrincham, Dunham (Massey) and Woodford, the latter apparently without permission of the landowner (17 December 1782). They often caught only one hare, and the most was five at Mottram. There is a reference to a lease of hares. Possibly this means three as a "leash" of hounds or hawks meant a group of three. (25 September 1783). See GAME LICENCE

HARE, JUGGED
Of two species eaten, the Scotch Blue and the English Brown, the latter is considered the better. The hare was hung in a cool cellar for several days to improve the flavour and tenderness, then placed in an earthenware pot (jug) with wild plums or crab apples and baked by burying in hot wood ashes.

HARROW'D
The drawing of a harrow, a heavy frame of timber (or iron) set with iron teeth, over ploughed land to break up the clods; to rake the soil or to cover seeds. (27 July 1786)

HATS
During the period of the diary large hats, adorned with bows and feathers, were fashionable. Examples of these can be seen in contemporary portraits by Thomas Gainsborough. The hair was often "frizzed" out.

HAVEYARD, ROBERT see CHEESE SELLING

HAY; ADDITION OF OTHER PLANTS
The sowing of **clover** and other **trefoils** with grass seed probably increased the yield of hay. See WINTER FEED

HAYING see HAYMAKING

HAYMAKING
Hay is made by cutting the grass grown in **meadows**. In July Peter **Pownall** sent his men to mow the grass with scythes (6 July 1786). An entry in the accounts of 1806 shows purchase of a new scythe from John Holt for 6s. **Casual labourers** were employed. The men cut the grass and left it on the ground to start drying. Then the women followed and turned over the swathes, tossing them to loosen the grass and allow it to dry through. When dry the grass was raked into piles and loaded onto hay wains or wagons and **lead** to the farm yard to be stacked. The whole process took about three weeks.

HAY, SALE OF
With the increase in the use of **horses** both on the farm where they took over from oxen and in towns for travelling and transport, new markets opened up for hay. Peter **Pownall** sold much of his hay crop. Some he sold in bulk, a stack at £40 to Messrs Blackshaw and Swin-

dells on 24 June 1807. Some he sold in smaller quantities to neigh- bours, friends, tenants and employees, like 1 cwt to Charles Leah for 4s in May 1793 and 18 cwt to **Mr Marsland** for £7 6s 0d in 1802 .

HEARERS
This refers to a **Presbyterian** congregation implying attenders rather than members.

HEARTH TAX
This tax was levied between 1662 and 1689. Those in receipt of poor **relief** and those who were excused poor rates were exempt, but all others had to pay 2s a year per hearth. The petty **constable** com- piled the lists of householders and their hearths. Records of this tax may be used to indicate social status or the size of the houses in a **township**. For example in Bramhall in 1674, of 87 houses listed the largest, that of William **Davenport**, lord of the manor, had 15 hearths. He also had a house with 4 hearths, possibly Mile End House. There were 3 other households with 3 hearths each and 7, including Elizabeth **Pownall**, had 2. Such houses probably had two living rooms - a "house" (the room used for cooking and eating) and a parlour. The other 47 houses had 1 hearth each only. Evidence of early tax payers up to 1689 can sometimes be found in **Subsidy Rolls**. The earliest such reference to the Pownall family is John Pownall who appears in the roll for 1641/2. See Appendix 5e & 5f

HEIFER
A young cow which has not **calved. (10 October 1782)**

HERIOT
This payment started in the Saxon period when the heir of a dead soldier had to return his armour to his lord. During Norman times this became a death duty payment to the lord of the manor, usually in the form of the best beast. References to heriots appear in leases, **inventories** and **court rolls** of the **Davenports**. The custom continued in Bramhall until the 17th century when the value of the beast varied from two or three to nine pounds. Towards the end of the century this became "best goods" and was later commuted to a money payment, usually five pounds.

HIGHWAY
Technically the right of way between two points such as towns, mark- ets, churches and **mills**, for travellers. This did not include side **roads** such as those between farms on the **manor**.

HIGHWAY; COMMUTATION OF SERVICE
Householders who were unable or unwilling to carry out their highway duties, could pay another to do so, or could make a payment to the **overseer of the highway**. With this he could employ other labourers. The payment varied but a cart and team could cost 4s, and one day's labour 2s.

HIGHWAY LAY
Highway lays (rates) were introduced by the Act of 1654 and supp- lemented statute labour. Peter **Pownall** paid William **Hallworth**, **overseer**, £1 12s 9d **(14 October 1782)**. In 1835 the Highways Act

abolished statutory labour.   Parishes were encouraged to form Highway Districts and appoint district surveyors.   The Act of 1866 made
the above compulsory and in 1888 maintenance of the main roads
became the duty of the county councils.   The rest of the roads were
adopted in 1894.

HIGHWAY MAINTENANCE
Under the 1555 Highways Act the responsibility for road maintenance
fell on the **parish** through which it ran.   In large parishes (most
common in the northwest) the responsibility was sub-divided between
townships.   From 1555 the churchwardens (or lords of the **manor)**
appointed four (later six) days on which all the inhabitants in the
parish had to turn out to work on repairing the highway.   Those who
had carts and draught animals had to produce them together with two
labourers.   Others had to bring their own tools and, under the
supervision of the **overseers** (sometimes called 'surveyors' or
'supervisors' of the **Highways)**, work at digging and loading gravel,
sand or stones onto carts at the pits, filling in potholes on the
roads or clearing **ditches** at the sides of the roads to aid drainage.
The Rolls for the **Court Baron** of Bramhall, midsummer 1640, contain
references ordering "the tenantes of Bramhall to Repeire the high
wais before St James day next sub penam [under penalty] of every
default 3s 4d ". They were ordered to "meete the **Overseer** of the
Highway at the **plat** above William Siddall's upon Saturday next or
the first faire day after by nyne of the Clocke of the same day to
do such work as they shall be appointed sub penam 1s separitum
[each] at Martinmas 1651". **(13 February 1783)**. See ROADS, SIDE OR
MINOR & SAINTS DAYS

HIGHWAY, OVERSEERS OF THE
In the 1285 Statute of Westminster the manorial obligation for the
upkeep of the King's **Highway** was made official, and was usually
under the supervision of a petty **constable**.   The 1555 Highways Act
stated that "two honest persons in each **parish** are to be elected
every year as surveyors or overseers of the highway".   They were
responsible for inspecting the state of the roads, for organising
and supervising repairs by their neighbours and fining those who
failed to do so.   This honorary office was very unpopular and every
householder had to serve for one year, so often a householder would
pay someone else to take his turn.   William **Hallworth**, elected in
1783, held the same office for at least three years and was probably
serving on behalf of others.   In Bramhall people seem to have served
in order of **houserow. (17 October 1783)**

HILLED
Possibly 'killed' the bees. See BEES, KEEPING

HIRING FAIRS
One of the earliest employment exchanges was at the local **fairs**,
known as hiring or mop fairs.   The applicants stood together each
wearing a token of his trade; a shepherd had a piece of wool, a
cowman a twist of cowhair and a gardener flowers in his hat.   The
farmer chose his worker, they agreed the wage and the contract was
sealed with a shilling.

HIVES see BEE HIVES

HOLED POTATOES see POTATOES, CULTIVATION OF

HOLIDAYS
Annual and Bank holidays are a recent development. In medieval times there were no such holidays but holy days were set apart for religious observance, usually to commemorate a saint. No work was done on these days and once the religious service was over the rest of the day was often celebrated with dancing, drinking and merry-making. Longer breaks in daily toil were enjoyed at Easter, Whitsun and Christmas, the last originally lasting twelve days. Many of the holy days were related to pre-Christian festivals. The Saxons cheered the shortest days by burning yule logs. Midsummer is reputed to owe its origins to the druids as also is Hallowe'en on 31 October. The church reacted to the latter by making the following day All Saints Day. See SAINTS DAYS

HOOPS
During the period of the diary hooped skirts were very fashionable. The skirts were distended sideways, sometimes for as much as fifteen feet, over a framework of whalebone or osier rods. This style was extremely inconvenient in confined areas.

HORSES
In Cheshire by this time horses were used in preference to oxen to pull ploughs. On light sandy soil two horses were sufficient to pull a plough but on heavy clay soil up to four horses were needed. They were also used for transport, on the farm for loads of **hay** and **corn**, and to draw wagons of goods to market or pull carriages and traps belonging to the family for business or pleasure. Peter **Pownall** was noted for his "powerful grey horses" and "powerful team" (of horses) which would have meant selective breeding. He also sold horses. References to horses include the paying of related taxes - **horse tax** and **saddle tax**. See appendix 5b

HORSE TAX
From 1784 to 1874 there was a tax on horses, with owners paying more for riding horses than for draught horses. Peter **Pownall** records buying a licence for his horse on **11 October 1784**. In May 1807 his

riding horse tax was £8, while his draught horses cost £1 17s 6d. We do not know how many horses he had. See SADDLE TAX

HOUSE OF CORRECTION
These were instituted under the English Poor Laws (1576 and 1597) in every county and city for the correction of the idle poor and the punishment of rogues. They were really penal institutions and the forerunners of modern prisons.

HOUSEROW
This was the system used in Bramhall to select the officers at the manor **court** to spread the liability of serving in a way which was perceived by the community as being fair. Householders took office in turn according to the house they lived in. For example in mid-summer 1634 William **Birch** served for Adshead's house as constable. In this way changes of tenancy did not affect the order of serving. It was possible to pay someone else to perform your office if you wished.

HOW LANE
One of the early forms of High Lane, a village between Hazel Grove and Disley. **(21 May 1787)**

HULME FAMILY
The first reference to this surname in Bramhall that we have found is the burial of Nicholas Hulme 1587/8. The family appears regularly in the **court rolls** and other local documents. There were Hulmes at Dog Hill Moor (1746 & 1848) and Dairyground (1767) in Bramhall and also a family in Woodford who had connections with **Dean Row chapel**. The Hulmes were related to the **Pownalls** by the first marriage of Peter Pownall's father, in 1750, to Jane Hulme of Bramhall. Their daughter, also called Jane, was born the following year, but her mother died soon after. The young Jane's uncle (possibly great-uncle) George Hulme of Lindow, Wilmslow was one of the first trustees of the **workhouse** there. He was also an appraiser of the **inventory** of Peter Pownall's great uncle, also Peter Pownall, who died in 1751. George Hulme is recorded in the diary **(2 November 1785)** as paying his niece Jane Pownall a "fortune" of £400. He died on 9 February 1787. A younger George Hulme is mentioned in the diary as being at Oxford from October to December 1782, and the following year marrying Sarah Partington **(3 June 1783)**. One Mr Hulme went hare coursing with Peter Pownall and his father **(5 November 1782)** and the ladies of the two families used to visit each other to drink tea. **(14 November 1782)**. See Appendix 6a

HUMPHREYS, SALUSBURY PRYCE, KNIGHT, RN, KCH, CB, JP
Was involved in the Chesapeake incident (1807), possibly one of the causes of the American War of Independence. In 1810 he married Maria **Davenport** becoming lord of the manor of Bramhall in 1829 in right of his wife on the death of her father. In 1838 he changed his name to Davenport by Act of Parliament.

HUNDRED
A subdivision of a county or shire, having its own court. There were seven hundreds in Cheshire. These were Broxton, Bucklow,

Eddisbury, Nantwich, Northwich, Wirral and Macclesfield. Bramhall was in the Macclesfield hundred, which was known as Hamestan in 1086. See COURT EYRE

INCLOSED
The earliest reference that we have found to the enclosure of land in Bramhall was before 1621. During the period of the diary **common land** was being divided up amongst the major land holders by consent. Each recipient had to fence his plot **(18 January 1787)**. There was no parliamentary enclosure act for Bramhall. See MOORS

INOCALATED see INOCULATION

INOCULATION
The introduction of the germs of an infectious disease through a puncture in the skin, in the hope that the body might develop a defence against more serious attacks of the disease. It was introduced to this country, against strong initial opposition, by Lady Mary Wortley Montague who learned of it in 1717 while living in Turkey, but was not recommended by the College of Physicians until 1754. In 1758 George Ridley, a Gloucestershire weaver, advertised his services in the Oxford Journal stating "it is no more than Scrattin a bit of a haul in their Yarm A pushin in a peece of Skraped rag dipt in sum of the Pocky Matter of a child under the distemper - that every Body in the Nashon may be sarved". Vaccination, using the much safer cowpox or vaccinia virus, was not introduced until 1786 by Edward Jenner, a country doctor also of Gloucestershire. Reports in the diary must refer to smallpox inoculation as it was not used for any other disease at this time. **(29 August 1783)**

INVENTORY
This was a list of all the possessions of a deceased person at the time of death, including furniture, etc. with valuation. The practice dates from Roman times but was a legal obligation from 1529. Many of those which have survived for Bramhall are at the Cheshire Record Office. See Appendix 5f

JONATHAN ROBERSONS see SCHOOL, ROBINSON'S

JP See JUSTICES OF THE PEACE

JUROR
A member of a jury. See COURT BARON

JUSTICES OF THE PEACE
These were first created as keepers of the peace in the 13th century to maintain law and order throughout the country. In 1348/9 the effects of the Black Death increased their duties. Later they were created justices of the peace (magistrates) and held **quarter sessions**, where they administered the acts of Parliament. Cheshire, as a county palatine, had no justices of the peace until the Act of 1536. During the Tudor period they were under the Privy Council and the Court of the Star Chamber. The Long Parliament (1640 - 1660) abolished the latter so the **Lords Lieutenant** and

sheriffs took over control of the JPs under the government. Any man holding land to the value of £20 per annum was eligible, but usually JPs were gentry or churchmen. There were a few with legal training. Starting with about six to eight per county their numbers increased to 50-60 in the 16th century.

JUSTICES OF THE PEACE; DUTIES
JPs were supposed to attend **Quarter Sessions** and were responsible for the area they represented. Each session in Cheshire generally lasted only one day. Usually 7-15 JPs attended the court for which they received 4s a day in expenses. But they had many other duties including road and bridge surveys; the issue of **licences** and **filiation orders**; authorising **relief**; suppressing illegal **ale houses** and occasionally riots.

KILL see MILL KILN

KILLED see DEATHS

KILLER, JOSHUA AND GEORGE
There are references in Heginbotham to a John Egerton Killer who came from Manchester in 1796 when he was appointed surgeon to the Stockport Cavalry. The next year he was a partner of Mr Briscall at the Free Dispensary. In 1831 this became the Stockport Infirmary **(20 November 1782)**. Killer is a common surname in the Nottingham area. **(25 November 1782)**

KITS MOSS see MOORS IN BRAMHALL

KNUTSFORD GAOL
Knutsford Gaol or **House of Correction** was built in 1817 as an additional county gaol to the one at Chester. It held between 180 and 280 persons, about one-fifth of whom were women. Only two-thirds of the inmates were convicted prisoners, the rest were awaiting trial at **Quarter Sessions**. The prison was run by a committee of **JPs**. It ceased to be used as a gaol sometime before the 1914-18 war. It was later a hostel and was demolished in 1934.

KNUTSFORD RACES see RACES

KNUTSFORD SESSIONS
Together with Chester this was one of the two centres for **Quarter Sessions** from 1760. The sessions house at Knutsford was repaired in the 1770s and in the early 19th century a new sessions house was built with a **house of correction** attached. Previously there had been a house of correction at Nantwich **(4 October 1785)**. At Knutsford Quarter Sessions in 1830 Sarah Hudson aged 20 and Ann Shaw aged 27 were accused of stealing a basket of wet clothes belonging to Peter **Pownall**. They were sentenced to twelve months hard labour.

LADY DAY see SAINTS' DAYS and QUARTER DAYS

LAID COWS IN
Young calves, oxen and milking cattle were brought under cover during the worst of the winter and kept tied up, usually two to a

stall in this area.   They were fed fodder.   Peter **Pownall** kept his stock inside from November to May. **(9 November 1782)**

LAMBS see SHEEP

LAY OR LEY
(1) A lay could be temporarily sown grassland used by the owner or rented out for grazing.   There were winter and summer lays.   The charges were per animal. Peter **Pownall** made a considerable income from the leasing of lays, "Recd: Mr Hatfield for **sheep lay** £17 19s 0d " (Accounts 12 May 1807).   He also seems to have leased them from other farmers, "Paid..Mr Ormrod 3 Lays at 1s 7d a lay for 2 Crofts in Cheadle Mosely for 1787 £0 4s 9d" (Accounts 12 May 1807)
(2) A rate or **tax**.   Among those paid by Peter Pownall and mentioned in the diary were the following:

Constable lay	to pay the expenses of the **petty constable** **(21 October 1783)**
Highway lay	for road maintenance **(14 October 1782)**. See HIGHWAY; COMMUTATION OF SERVICE.
Moor lay	in Bramhall for the grazing of animals on the **moors** or possibly for the right of **turbary** – the cutting of **peat** **(10 July 1783)**
Poor lay	for the **relief** of the **poor** (Accounts 16 December 1807) See MOORLOOKER

Other references include John Hallworth who had not paid his lays when he died **(25 December 1782)**. As the meeting was at James **Goulden's**, who was the **farmer** of **tithes**, this lay may have been a **tithe**.

LAY GROUNDS
The rotation method of cultivation in Cheshire included the periodic ploughing up of pasture land. **(11 March 1783)**.   See LAY & ROTATED CROPS

LEADING
The local dialect word "leading" was used to describe both the loading of the carts in the field and leading the horses to the farmyard where the crop was unloaded **(4 October 1782)**.   Peter **Pownall** also lead in **hay** from the **meadows** **(15 July 1786)**.

LEASE see HARE COURSING

LICENCE, ALE SELLING see ALE SELLING LICENCE

LICENCE FOR CARTS see CART TAX

LICENCE FOR ONE HORSE see HORSE TAX

LICENCE TO KILL GAME see GAME LICENCE

LIME AS A SOIL IMPROVER
Lime is one of the oldest chemicals used in agriculture.   It is known to have been made in Buxton by the Romans.   It is produced by heating limestone (calcium carbonate) to drive off carbon dioxide and leave quick lime (calcium oxide).   This is a caustic substance

that combines readily with water to form slaked lime (calcium hydroxide). It is only at this stage that it can be used in agriculture. During the 18th century the agricultural revolution increased its use. It was expensive due to the high cost of transport. In 1752 the recommended dressing of two tons per acre every twenty years cost £2 14s 0d. In 1796 the Peak Forest Canal Company, of which Samuel **Oldknow** was a considerable shareholder, opened a canal. It was connected to the Peak Forest Tramway, which carried limestone down from Doveholes to Buxworth, in 1799. From here the stone was taken by canal to Marple to be burnt in Oldknow's lime kilns. This reduced the cost of lime to one fifth. We do not know where Peter **Pownall** purchased his lime **(30 April 1783)**. He used it on his land **(25 June 1783)**.

LIME; OTHER USES
Lime was also used around the farm to clean and sweeten wooden utensils like churns and buckets, or mixed with coarse fat and water to make lime wash, a medieval waterproof "emulsion paint". It was also used in the process of tanning skins. Today it is largely used in the chemical industry.

LIVE
Possibly Mary Brown was engaged as a living-in servant. **(3 November 1783)**. See FARM WORKERS

LIVERPOOL
During the 17th century Liverpool's trade increased and diversified, which brought prosperity to the town. By 1705 Defoe described it as "one of the wonders of Britain" with its handsome new buildings. In the 18th century the African slave trade added to its wealth; goods that were suitable for barter, such as cloth, spirits and household utensils, were taken to the Guinea coast and exchanged for slaves. These were taken to America (the West Indies) to be sold and, with the profits, sugar and tobacco were bought and shipped to Liverpool. The slave trade was abolished in 1807. Another important cargo was raw cotton from the Southern States. Liverpool must have been an exciting place to visit whether for business or pleasure. **(15 May 1787)**

LOAD
A load of **oatmeal** at this time weighed 240lbs **(4 October 1782)**. See WEIGHTS and MEASURES

LORD LIEUTENANT
Usually a peer or great landowner in charge of a county. He was appointed by the Crown from Tudor times, his main duty being to see to the military strength of his county. This he largely delegated to his deputies. See MILITIA

LYING IN
Giving birth to a child. **(4 May 1784)**. See DEATHS

MACCLESFIELD FOREST see FOREST, MACCLESFIELD

MACCLESFIELD HUNDRED see HUNDRED

MACCLESFIELD RACES

Macclesfield had a race course in the early 19th century. It was in a field near the old toll bar on London Road. Later a new course was built in the West Park, opened in October 1828. The meetings were held twice a year during **Wakes** week and **Barnaby**. They were discontinued after a fatal accident in 1853. Mr W C **Brocklehurst**, Sarah **Pownall's** grandson, was a steward in 1852. **(7 October 1783)**. See RACES

MAHOGANY CHAIRS

Mahogany was imported from the Americas. It is a strong, fine-grained wood that is especially suitable for table tops and chairs with pierced and carved backs. Although we do not know the style of the ten chairs Peter **Pownall** bought, he would have a good selection to choose from as this was the period of Chippendale, Hepplewhite, Sheraton and Adam, when chairs were delicate and elegant. **(21 December 1782)**. See CARPET

MAHOGANY CHAIRS c1775-1790.

MALT

The best malt is made from **barley**. In its natural state the starch is insoluble in water, so useless for brewing, but during germination an enzyme converts the starch into a soluble form which a brewer makes into a sugar solution. This process is called "mashing". The germinating of barley is called "malting". The barley is soaked for 60 hours and then dried by spreading it several inches thick on the malting floor called "flooring". The barley germinates and has to be turned several times to prevent the sprouts matting. After a period of time the maltster halts the process and the malt is dried in the kiln. It is then milled to crack the grains ready for **brewing**. Peter **Pownall** quoted the value of malt at 40s per load **(5 October 1782)** and sent as much as 32 measures of barley to the kiln at one time **(14 March 1784)**. The kiln was at Dean Row near Wilmslow, and payments were made to a Mr Norbury for malting. See MILL KILN

MANCHESTER ACADEMY

Originally the Warrington Acadamy, this **Unitarian** school was founded there in 1757 and moved to Manchester in June 1783. There it prospered as the Manchester College. In 1803 the acadamy moved to York, returning to Manchester in 1840. It was described as the "fountain head of Unitarian learning in England" and attracted students from home and abroad. Its last move was to London in 1853. **(5 October 1786)**

MANCHESTER FAIRS see FAIRS, MANCHESTER

MANCHESTER RACES see RACES

STOCKPORT MARKET c. 1800.

MANOR
An area of land held by a lord. The **Davenport** family owned the manor of Bramhall from around 1370 to 1877. The manors surrounding Bramhall were Stockport, Handforth-cum-Bosden, Norbury, Poynton, Woodford and Cheadle.

MANOR COURT see COURT BARON

MANUREING see MUCKING

MARE
Female horse. **(17 March 1783).** See HORSES

MARKED SHEEP
When sheep were grazed on **common** pasture it was necessary to distinguish your sheep from your neighbours' flocks. Peter Pownall used his initial "P", possibly by branding with a hot iron. Today most sheep are marked with coloured dye on the fleeces to show ownership. **(15 October 1782)**

MARKET GARDENING
The growing of **vegetables** for sale.

MARKET GARDENING; PETER POWNALL
Peter **Pownall** practised several different types of farming; the keeping of stock, the growth of cereal products and a wide range of specialist products not usually associated with farming. Today the latter are grown by market gardeners. His crops included **asparagus**, beans (kidney and unnamed varieties), broccoli, cabbages (winter and savoys), **carrots**, cauliflowers, celery, lettuces, onions, parsley, peas and radishes. He also grew fruit including apples, currants and gooseberries **(8 April 1783)**. The populations of the local towns of Stockport and Macclesfield were growing with the development of industry and would have provided a ready market for such produce.

MARKET, STOCKPORT
From medieval times markets were usually held once a week, and gave
local people an opportunity to sell their surplus products and to
buy things they could not grow or make. By 1680 Stockport market-
place was an open area with a cross raised on six steps, a conduit
for water, a market house, a butchers' shambles at the west side and
a public meal house to the east. Then it was a "considerable market
for **corn** and provisions". By the 18th century it was noted for
cheese and **oatmeal**. The tolls were paid to the lord of the manor.
In 1645 they amounted to £30 14s 2d and in 1730 £89 13s 10d. In
1883 they had risen to £1,879 19s 4d but by then the manorial rights
had been sold to the Corporation (1850). In 1835 the market was
considered too small and the New Market was built for potatoes
behind the Old Admiral Inn on Middle Hillgate, now demolished. It
was never opened due, it is said, to lack of a licence. There was a
cattle market in Great Portwood Street from 1878 to 1936. The present covered market was erected in 1861 with open sides; these were
enclosed in 1898. See FAIRS, STOCKPORT.

MARL
This was a form of naturally occurring fertiliser used from the 14th
century by farmers in Cheshire to bring waste land into cultivation.
It is a calcareous clayey substance deposited by the glaciers onto
the Cheshire plain. This clay was dug from marl pits and spread
over the ground. It is easily crumbled and washed into the earth by
the rain. It added body to sandy soils and, possibly, fertility to
mosses. Its benefit on clay soil was questioned in the old Cheshire
rhyme "He that marls sand may buy the land; he that marls moss shall
have no loss; he that marls clay flings all away". Bramhall leases
contain references to "marling" of the land. In his lease for 1674
William **Birch** agreed to take marl for composting and manuring. Ten
years before, John Brown's lease obliged him to marl his new closes
(inclosed land) called Dairy Meadows. This was repeated in 1698
when he had the right to dig or take marl. See MARL PITS

MARLERS
Sometimes marl was dug and carted by travelling gangs of marlers.
Not surprisingly the occasion became an excuse for fun. Some descr-
iptions tell of **bull-baiting** in the pit, maypole and sword dancing
and feasting in the hall or barn.

MARL PITS
The Bramhall Tithe (1842) shows a large number of marl pits. Even
today remains can be found as ponds. Stella Davies wrote that marl
was found in pockets often just below the surface of the ground.
Each pit had a sloping side where wagons entered for loading, and a
vertical face where excavation took place. The pits used to fill
with water and could be a danger to people travelling cross country
especially after dark. There are records of people drowning in marl
pits.

MARPLE see ESTATES

MARRIED
Although Peter **Pownall** himself remained a bachelor all his life his

diary contains references to 19 marriages. Two of these we quote below as examples of the period, one a farm labourer and the other a gentry wedding.

MARRIED, JOSEPH SHAW

Joseph Shaw and Jenny Glave were married on 5 June 1783, probably after a typical country courtship. This used to take place by the kitchen fire after the family had gone to bed on a Saturday night and was known as the "sitting up". In northern England it was customary to exchange betrothal rings formed of two links or loops called "gemmel" rings. On the wedding day the best man led the bride to the **parish** church and the bridegroom led the bridesmaid. They would return home after the ceremony with bride and groom together, the families having remained at work in the fields and home. There was usually some feasting afterwards. See WEDDING CLOTHES

MARRIED, SISTER SARAH

Sarah married Mr John **Brocklehurst** on 27 March 1783. This would have been a grand wedding and although they were members of **Dean Row Unitarian Chapel** they would not have been married there. Until 1837 all marriages had to take place at the **parish** church. The ceremony was similar to today's but there were bridemen as well as bridemaids (sic). The bride carried a posy and the men had flowers in their buttonholes, but flowers were also strewn in the path of the bride. By the 18th century the wedding ring was worn on the left hand. One custom was the passing of a piece of wedding cake through the ring. Bachelors and spinsters who ate it believed that they too would soon be married. Afterwards there would have been a feast and then the bridal couple were escorted to bed, after which the guests continued their revellings. It seems likely that the happy couple went on a honeymoon (a rare occurrence) for it was nearly three months before Sarah made her **appearance** at **Dean Row** (**15 June 1783**). See CARPET and WEDDING CLOTHES & Appendices 6a & 6b

MARSLAND, JOHN

There was a John Marsland living in Stockport at this time. He died on 27 December 1811 at the age of 62. **(15 January 1784)**

MARSLAND, MR, OF BULLOCK SMITHY

Henry Marsland was a cotton manufacturer in **Bullock Smithy** (now Hazel Grove). His house and the adjoining mill stood on the south corner of Queens Road. His sons, Samuel and Peter, extended the premises and Peter later built Woodbank Hall. It is possible that the dance was held at Henry **Marsland's**. **(5 November 1788)**

MARTINMAS DAY, NEW see NEW CALENDAR & QUARTER DAYS

MASSEY see TIMBER

MEADOWS

In 1795 Aiken wrote that three quarters of Cheshire was "pastured" or mown. The lush meadows, frequently near to a stream, were kept to grow grass for hay-making. Pastures were less good areas, including low hillsides, where cattle were grazed during summer months. See LAY OR LEY

MEAL
This is the edible part of any grain (usually excepting wheat) or
pulse, ground into a powder or small flakes, eg **oatmeal**. It can
also be used as coarse flour. The local **mill** was used to grind
animal foodstuffs as well as grain for human consumption. Peter
Pownall makes frequent references to the price of meal which he
sells and which appears from the accounts to fluctuate in price considerably. For example on 19 August 1791 it was 25s 6d per **load**; on
1 August 1793, 50s; and on 29 August 1794, 32s 9d. **(4 October 1782)**

METHODISM AND PETER POWNALL
The first reference to Methodism in Bramhall is to a meeting in
Jeremiah Royle's house in 1743. About the beginning of the 1800s
Peter **Pownall** was asked to fit up a barn, built onto a cottage in
Benja Fold, as a chapel but he declined. He also refused to sell
any of his land for them to build on. The Pownalls were prominent
members of **Dean Row** Unitarian Chapel.

BENJA FOLD.

MICHAELMAS DAY see SAINTSDAYS and QUARTER DAYS

MILITIA
Originally the "Fyrd" or military force formed of freemen to
serve their Anglo-Saxon kings, it developed into a citizen's aux-
iliary army. During the Tudor period the system was reorganised.
The **Lord Lieutenant** was nominal head of his county militia but he
delegated most of his responsibilities to his deputies. It was the
constable who had to raise the levy and look after the equipment.
Each **township** had to provide a set number of soldiers. All men
between 18 and 45 were eligible and were selected by ballot, but a
substitute could be paid. The men had to attend training sessions.
At the beginning of the 18th century they were paid 1s 6d per day.

When this was cut to 6d in 1757 there were riots in Stockport. In 1811 more than 1000 men were drilled on **Sandy Brow**. The wives and families of serving men could apply for **relief**. Joseph **Shaw** had presumably finished his term of service. **(18 March 1783)**

MILK, "BEGUN A SELLING"

Until the industrial revolution and the resulting population growth in the towns, sufficient milk could usually be obtained from cows kept in the towns (even in the centre of London). The sudden increase in demand encouraged milk production and sale, but there are no further references to milk sales in the diary or accounts. We know that milk was sent to Stockport from the surrounding villages, probably in churns on carts since the carrying of milk on packhorses, when it slopped in rhythm with the animal's movements, tended to produce butter on arrival! After the 1840s milk was easily transported by train. **(20 May 1786)**

MILL

A mill was a necessity in every area and could be powered by water or wind. They were very expensive to set up and maintain and usually belonged to the lord of the **manor**. Bramhall had a mill on the river Brame (now Ladybrook) in an area off Valley Road, known locally as Happy Valley. It was powered by a water wheel fed by a leet from a mill pond with a weir. Every tenant was obliged to "grind all his .. **corn** or grain of whatever nature or kind .. which shall be used upon the .. premises at the milne". Other produce ground there included beans and peas. The lord usually 'farmed' the running of the mill, ie. accepted an annual lump sum from the miller who, in Bramhall, was entitled to keep one sixteenth of all the grain he ground as his remuneration. Such a system led to widespread abuse as in the folksong the "Miller of Dee". Our millers were no exception; in 1636 one was ordered "to take speciall care that he suffer not the wandringe boy John Kitchen (usually called Cashe) nor any other idle wandringe persons to frequent the Millne". In 1647 the miller was accused by the tenants of not grinding the corn promptly when it was brought to the mill "though he have very little to do". The lords and millers seem to have continued their uneasy relationships for it is said that early in the 19th century, after an argument with the then miller, Mr Hampson, over repairs, the lord unroofed the mill and let it fall into decay. In 1850 the water power, sufficient for two mills, was advertised to let. See FARMER

MILLER, BETTY

Betty Miller probably lived in one of Peter **Pownall's** houses. **(18 December 1782)**

MILL KILN

A kiln was usually part of, or near to, a mill. The grain was spread on a perforated tile floor over a fire to dry before grinding. The kiln at Bramhall was burned down in October 1702 while being used to dry hemp. It must have been rebuilt as it was mentioned in deeds of 1717. A kiln can be seen at Nether Alderley Mill. See BARLEY and MALT

MILL LEET

This was an open channel to conduct water to the mill wheel. In Bramhall it was cut through sand and the banks had to be protected against erosion. A hurdle-like framework was fixed to the banks and the space behind filled with earth. This was known as a "gripyard". The maintenance and repair of the mill stream in the 17th century was the responsibility of all the householders. In 1637, at a summer meeting of the **manor court**, they were ordered to "meete this daie three weekes the xxixth [29th] of July at Woman's Croft **Bridge** [on Bridge Lane] to amende the gripyard". But by 1716 the responsibility for the leet fell on "all people with lands lying at the water side betwixt the weir and womanscroft bridge where the beaches are". They were ordered to secure the lord's land in **paine** of 13s 4d. In 1723 eighteen people were ordered to clean out the mill **ditch** and again in 1728 "to dress their parts of the mill ditch".

MOOR LAYS see LAY OR LEYS and MOORLOOKER

MOORLOOKER

Every year the Bramhall **manor court** appointed four householders, one to superintend the use of each moor. Their duties included controlling the number of **cattle** grazing there **(stinting)**, seeing that fences and **ditches** were in order, checking the boundaries and, by the end of the 18th century, collecting moor **lays** (a form of tax for the use of the moor). Moorlookers were chosen by **houserow**, although it was possible to pay another to carry out the duty. For example in 1643 Richard Smith acted on behalf of "Widdow Leigh" on Bramhall Moor. In 1728 William **Pownall** was moorlooker for Kitts Moor, and one of his ancestors, John Pownall, had held the same office in 1632. **(10 July 1783)**. See COURT OFFICIALS AND THEIR DUTIES

MOORS OR MOSSES

These were beds of peat that had formed in shallow basins hollowed out by glacial drift and filled with decaying vegetable matter, which had then died due to a combination of poor drainage and cold weather. As wood became scarce in the medieval period peat was used as fuel. Surveys were made of peat beds, boundaries were defined between neighbouring manors, and **moorlookers** were appointed. All of Bramhall's moors share boundaries with the moors of other manors. Each **commoner** was allocated a share (a strip or strips) which became known as **moss rooms**. The right to cut turf or **peat** is known as the right of **turbary**.

MOORS IN BRAMHALL

There were four moors or mosses, in Bramhall - Bramhall Moor, Doghill Moor, Kitts Moss and Snybbs (or Snybbes) Moor. Bramhall was bounded by Bramhall Moor Lane, the A6 in Hazel Grove, Hatherlow Lane and a line to Rutters Lane. Doghill was shared with Woodford and is now the Bramhall Golf Course. Kitts Moss was approximately the land enclosed by Ack Lane, Moss Lane, Ford's Lane and Kitts Moss Lane. Snibbs Moor was shared with Stockport and probably included Woodsmoor and across the A6 to Mile End (Stockport School). The Stockport part extended as far as Dialstone Lane and included Stockport Great Moor.

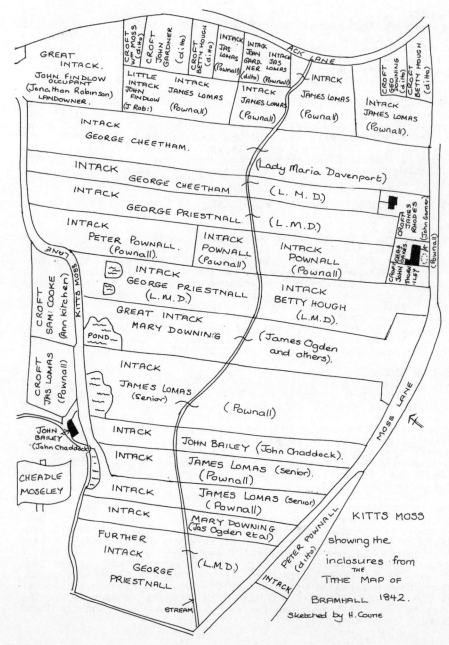

KITTS MOSS

showing the

inclosures from THE

TITHE MAP OF

BRAMHALL 1842.

Sketched by H. Coune

MOORS, RECLAMATION OF
As early as 1656 William Smith wrote of the reclamation of Cheshire mosses (moors). In 1716 J Mortimer described the process in Bowdon, where one John Edmunds added 600 cartloads of sand to his moss. The next year it was **dunged** and created a good **meadow**. He reckoned to have improved the value of the land from 10s to £6 per acre. In another area he used a **breast plough** to clear the turf which was burned on the site. Then the land was ploughed and used to grow **barley**. After the peat had been cut from the Bramhall **moss rooms** the tenants reclaimed the land which resulted in the series of long narrow shaped fields shown on the 1842 **tithe map** of Bramhall. In 1666 John Amery's lease (for land from William **Davenport**) described how the moss room was to be reclaimed. "For bettering of the soyle thereof .. cut down and burn brooms, gorse, underwoods and brushes coming or growing or increasing in or any part of the moss .. to the development of the land."

MOSS ROOM
The first reference to moss rooms in Stockport was in a "Moss Roll Book" dated 1556. It described a long narrow strip of the peat moss on the moor. The sizes of rooms varied but Peter Ridgway owned one of 190 yards by 7 yards on Kitts Moss in 1719. The rooms were allocated .to all who enjoyed right of **commons** and after they were **inclosed** owners would exchange them to rationalise their holdings and make them more convenient to farm. Peter **Pownall** Snr. exchanged such a room with Robert **Hardy**. **(24 January 1785)**

MOWING see HAYMAKING

MUCKING
The spreading of farmyard manure over the meadows and fields to enrich the soil, which was often obligatory in Bramhall leases. **(6 August 1783)**

MURRAY, MR AND MRS
Probably Mary and Nathaniel Murray, Peter Pownall's uncle and aunt. Mrs Murray died in 1788. **(18 September 1784 & 15 August 1788)**. See Appendix 6a

MZTD
We cannot read this word. We think it may be a form of "mazered," a northern dialect word meaning stupified or delirious. In the first three months of every year Peter Pownall bought between two and four **store pigs** which he fattened and then either sold or slaughtered in November or December. Judging from the date it is possible that this pig was sick with a form of meningitis, one cause of which was the high salt content of preserved waste food fed to pigs. The symptoms made a pig walk in circles, bang its head against walls and at times exhibit a wild frenzy. **(11 January 1787)**

NEW CALENDAR
The Julian Calendar (named after Julius Caesar) was devised in 45 BC. It had 365 days but to balance it an extra day was added to every fourth year, making a solar year of 365 1/4 days. This was not accurate and the errors accumulated so that in 1582 Pope Gregory

XIII ordered the use of a reformed (Gregorian) calendar which omitted ten days (5-14 October) in that year. He also ordered each year to begin on 1 January instead of 25 March. This calendar was not adopted in England until Chesterfield's Act of 1751. This decreed that 1752 began on 1 January and, to conform with the Gregorian calendar, that 2 September should be followed by 14 September. Many people felt they had lost eleven days of their lives. Even thirty years later Peter Pownall noted the occurrence of old **Michaelmas Day**. (11 November & 22 November 1782)

NEW MARTINMAS see NEW CALENDAR

NEW MICHAELMAS DAY see NEW CALENDAR

NONCONFORMIST
One who refused to conform with the practices of the Church of England but remained a member. After 1662 those who refused to accept the Act of Uniformity left the established church.

NORBURY WAKES see WAKES, NORBURY

OATMEAL
Ground **oats** used for human food such as porridge or oatcake. Aiken, writing in 1795, told of great quantities of corn and oatmeal being sold at Stockport **market**. See MEAL

OATS
Oats were one of the main cereal crops grown in Cheshire at this time and formed nearly half of Peter **Pownall's** cereal crop in 1842. Oats were used as food for humans as **oatmeal**, and were crushed for **horses**. Peter Pownall wrote of sowing oats in April after ploughing the ground, and **leading** his oats after harvest (5 October 1782). He **threshed** them throughout the winter (**18 October 1783 & 16 March 1784**). He sold oats to many customers, including friends and neighbours, apparently to feed horses.

OLD FOLD FARM
At the end of Grosvenor Street, Hazel Grove, stands Old Fold Farm. A date stone shows that the house was rebuilt in 1878 by P P B[rocklehurst], who probably received it with the rest of the Pownall **estates**. Recent alterations have revealed a timber framework probably of the 16th-17th century. See Appendix 5c & 6a

OLDKNOW, SAMUEL (1756-1828)
He came to Stockport around 1784 and purchased a house and warehouse on Hillgate. There he manufactured fine muslins, employing over 300 hand-loom weavers. He left Stockport in 1790 and settled in Marple where he opened a mill and built an apprentice house for the 90 orphaned girls he employed. He had many other interests which included agriculture (he experimented with new ideas), coal mining, and the building of turnpike roads and canals, the latter connected with the transport and manufacture of **lime**. In 1824 he was High Sheriff of Derbyshire. He was known as a "kind and considerate" landlord and employer but his interests over-stretched his resources and he died a poor man.

OLD MICHAELMAS DAY see NEW CALENDAR

OLD SWITHIN'S DAY
St Swithin's Day is 15 July. Some believe that if it rains on that
day there will be rain for forty days. Swithin was Bishop of Winchester and died in 862. **(26 July 1783)**. See NEW CALENDAR and
SAINTS' DAYS

OUTDOOR RELIEF
The giving of **relief** to the deserving poor outside the **workhouse**.
The system was thought to be open to abuse and several Poor Laws
attempted to compel the poor to live in a workhouse before receiving relief.

OVERSEER OF THE HIGHWAYS see HIGHWAY, OVERSEER OF

OVERSEER OF THE POOR see POOR, OVERSEER OF

PAIN[E]
Punishment, penalty or a fine. See COURT ROLLS, SOME COMMONLY USED
WORDS

PARISH
A parish was the area served by a parson.   Those living within the
parish paid **tithes** to him. In the northwest of England many parishes were very large.   Stockport parish included fourteen separate
townships and contained 25,175 **acres**. The parish church has stood
on the site of the present **St Mary's** in the market place since the
14th century. In the 19th century the ancient parishes were divided
into smaller units and many new churches were built.   In 1825 Bramhall became a part of the new parish of St Thomas but it was not
until 1911 that the new parish of Bramhall, St Michael and All
Angels, was created.

PARISH VESTRY
Gradually the **parish** became an area of secular administration under
the parish vestry, especially during the 15th and 16th centuries. It
had always been responsible for collecting and administering the
church rate but later it took over other duties such as the **relief**
of the poor and **highway maintenance**. Under the 1662 Act the **township** rather than the parish was the poor law unit in Cheshire and
Lancashire.   In 1894 local government reform replaced the vestry
with an elected parish council which had to meet at least once a
year.

PARTRAIGE
Partridge, a game bird. **(27 January 1783)**

PASTURE see MEADOWS

PEAS see MARKET GARDENING

PEAT see MOORS OR MOSSES

PEAT CUTTING
Peat was cut during the summer months. Towards the end of April the
surface grass was skimmed off and the men cut the peat beneath with
a narrow spade, into brick shaped pieces.   A good worker could cut
1,000 pieces a day. The peat was soft so the "bricks" were laid out
to dry by the women and children. In dry weather the peat would be
ready to stand on end after two weeks, and later it was piled into
mounds ready to be carted home and stacked for use as winter fuel.
One family could burn as many as 15,000 peats during a winter. Peat
had other uses; as bedding for cattle, dyeing wool and leather, and
even as a mattress for babies as it soaked up moisture and acted as
a deodorant! See MOSSROOM

PETTY CONSTABLE see CONSTABLE, PETTY

PETTY SESSIONS
From the 16th century monthly court sessions of J.P.s were held in
each **hundred**.   Macclesfield was split into two petty sessional
divisions, Prestbury and Stockport, a third, Hyde, was created about
1848.

PHALLOWING see FALLOWING

PICKFORD'S COTTON SHOP
There was a Mr Pickford at Birches Farm, now called High Stacks, at
Poynton. He is known to have employed hand-loom **silk weavers** and it
is possible he was associated with Pickfords removal firm. The reference in the diary may be to a burglary. **(4 November 1785)**

PIE POWDER see COURT OF PIE POWDER

PIGS
There are several terms for pigs; for example a hog or boar, a male
pig reared for slaughter; and a shoot, a young pig between the age
of a suckling pig and a fully grown one **(26 December 1782)**. Pig
keeping on a large scale was not practised in Bramhall but most
householders kept one or two pigs to fatten for winter food.   These
were known as "store pigs".   The four month old piglets were bought
in spring, or even earlier, and allowed to range on the common or
scavenge near the house.   These were slaughtered during the following winter and the meat preserved by smoking or salting. It was not
until the 19th century that pigs were kept in styes.   **(14 March
1783)**. See MZTD

PINFOLD
An enclosed area for confining stray or **distrained** animals. The
Bramhall pinfold was said to have been near the park gates on
Bramhall Green.   It was later moved to the side of Bridge Lane
between the present day roundabout and Valley Road, but it was dis-
mantled about 1884. See COURT OFFICIALS AND THEIR DUTIES, Pinder.

PLAT(T)
A local name for a small bridge.

PLAY

We do not know whether Peter **Pownall** attended the play in Manchester or Stockport. Touring companies performed tragedies, comedies and pantomimes wherever suitable premises and an audience could be found. The earliest reference to plays in Manchester was a play bill circa 1743. In 1789 an advertisement for the Theatre Royal, Manchester showed a double bill, a tragedy and a farce. Between the acts, songs and duets were performed. **(11 August 1785** and **13 May 1789)**

PLOUGH MONDAY

The first Monday after Twelfth Night was the day when the ploughs were blessed but the festival rapidly became an excuse for merry making. The ploughmen dressed up and took their ploughs from house to house. Should a householder fail to provide a gift his front path could be ploughed up! Another Monday reference found is to "Saint Monday" which was not a church festival, but a term used by those who overindulged on a Sunday and were unable to go to work on the Monday!

POINTON PARK see POYNTON PARK and WARREN FAMILY

POOR, ACCOUNTS OF THE OVERSEER OF THE

The detailed accounts kept by the **overseers of the poor** can be of use to local historians. The Bramhall Township Book for the period of the diary includes accounts for the highways, the constable and the relief of the poor. The combination of the accounts for the three offices became common about this time. The **township** was divided into several areas including **Bullock Smithy** and Siddall. Payments were made to the unemployed, the sick, widows (especially of the **militia**), orphans and bastard children (See FILIATION ORDERS). Doctors' fees for treatment and medicines, contributions to the **poor house** in Charlestown (probably a cottage) and to the **workhouse** at Millgate Hall were paid annually. The money was collected as **poor lays** from all residents of Bramhall. The accounts were submitted annually for checking, for example on 26 March 1822 when the meeting was held at a local inn, "the house of George Goddard at the sign of the Dog and Partridge in Bramhall".

POORHOUSE

This was the earliest form of **workhouse**. The poorhouse, often a small cottage, was bought or erected with money from the **poor lays** to house the incapacitated poor. It was supervised by the overseer of the poor, who was supposed to provide raw materials so that the residents could work to help to support themselves (under the Act of 1597/8, revised 1601). The poorhouse for Bramhall was at Charlestown.

POOR LAYS (LEYS)

Every householder had to contribute to the cost of providing for the aged, impotent poor, orphans and unemployed in their township. This tax was called the poor lay, and the money was disbursed by the overseers of the poor. To reduce the cost, from 1662, relief was only given to those who had a **settlement** in the township. Peter **Pownall** entered his payments from 1806 to 1808 in his accounts.

POOR, OVERSEER OF THE

The origins of this office date back to the time of Edward III when alms were collected for the poor. The re-organisation of the poor law during the reign of Elizabeth I required the appointment of two people from each **parish** to collect alms from their neighbours at church, distribute them and keep accounts. From 1572 an overseer was elected annually by the **Vestry** to supervise the collectors, whose honorary duties included finding work for the poor to perform in return for **relief**. By 1598 duties were increased to include giving weekly relief to the blind, aged and impotent poor, keeping a stock of work materials for the able-bodied poor, housing the destitute, providing education or apprenticeships for pauper chidren, and administering charitable bequests. Detailed accounts had to be kept. From 1722 **parishes** (or **townships**) were encouraged to build **workhouses**. The Poor Law Amendment Act 1834 was intended to abolish **outdoor relief** and subject paupers to the workhouse test. This was not always practicable, as for example during the cotton famine (1862-5) when 30,000 were unemployed in Stockport and the workhouse could only hold 500-600. To control the system locally Guardians of the Poor were elected and they employed Relieving Officers. Peter **Pownall** Snr. was an overseer of the poor for the year 1783/4. Nearly a year later a summons was served on him for failing to pay in the balance of money which he held at the end of his term of office **(23 April 1784** and **1 February 1785)**. During the year 1821/22 our Peter Pownall served with John **Fallows** and John **Hallworth** as overseers of the poor. At a meeting held in the Three Tuns, Hazel Grove each year, overseers were elected and sworn in before two local **JPs**; that year they were Capt. Salusbury Pryce **Humphreys** and Peter **Marsland**.

POTATO BOWS see POTATOES, CULTIVATION OF

POTATOES

The common potato was brought to Europe from South America about 1580. Sir Walter Raleigh probably brought the sweet potato from Virginia, but it had been known in 1589 when it was described as a "most delicious root". By the end of the 18th century the common potato was no longer considered a delicacy and was becoming an alternative to bread as a basic food. It was being grown in Cheshire by 1770 but "not extensively" according to Arthur Young. It was the shortage of food during the Napoleonic wars and the growing population that led to potatoes becoming a field crop.

POTATOES, CULTIVATION OF

Peter Pownall records "setting" (planting) potatoes in March, April and May. There is a tradition among gardeners of planting potatoes at Easter which would account for sowing at the first two dates. The potato has to be "earthed up" as it grows to protect the tubers from light which turns them green and poisonous. Could these ridges be potato bows? **(3 May 1784)**. Early potatoes may have been ready to harvest in June when Peter Pownall refers to ploughing **(30 June 1784)** and "getting potatoes" **(26 June 1787)**. The main crop may have been sown in May **(10 May 1784)** and harvested in October **(14 October 1782)** when he began "to get up potatoes for keeping". The main crop was stored for winter use by piling them up, covering with straw and then soil to form "clamps". It is possible that this is the meaning of "holed" **(24 October 1782)**. "New potatoes" for Christmas could be kept by burying in a container until required. In winter the potato ground was ploughed and drawn into **butts (12 November 1782)**.

POTATOES IN BRAMHALL

It was thought that growing potatoes exhausted the soil, so early leases contained a clause to limit the amount of potatoes that could be grown in any one year to that required to feed the family and servants. In 1749 John **Benison** could not "Digg Delve or Set with potatoes any more of the said Demised Premises than shall be used in his .. family."

POTATO GROUNDS

As well as growing potatoes for sale and family use Peter Pownall appears to have rented potato grounds to others. In his accounts for 1808 he recorded "Recd Peter Brown for potatoe ground £1.12s."

POWNALL, ALICE (1768-1831)

Peter's sister Alice, or "Ally", features several times in the diary. She went to school in Manchester **(21 July & 21 Dec 1784)** and visited the **Stockport Assembly** with Mr **Worthington (12 January 1783, 3 February & 3 March 1787)**. She died a spinster and, according to Burton, was "out of her mind".

POWNALL COTTAGES see RENT

POWNALL FAMILY

We have found evidence of Pownalls living in Bramhall since the early 15th century and it is probable that they were related to the Pownalls of Pownall Hall, Wilmslow. The first references are to Edmund and Robert who were land-holders and jurors in the 1440s. In 1518 another Robert Pownall, accused of murdering Ottiwell Booth in Stockport market place, was helped to escape justice by several of his Bramhall neighbours, including Thomas **Birch** and Richard Davenport.
Peter Pownall's ancestors may have included Humphrey Pownall whose natural son John inherited before his legitimate offspring, and John, Humphrey and Francis Pownall who signed the remonstrance to William Davenport in 1642, refusing to follow their lord in his support of the Royalist cause during the Civil War. Francis later became wagon master to Col. Henry Bradshaw's company at the battle of Worcester in 1651.
Peter Pownall's great grandfather, according to Thomas Turner (Burton mss.) had been a merchant in London and had built Pownall Hall. This appears to be the time when the family began purchasing land from their landlords, the **Davenports**. See Appendices 5 & 6a

POWNALL HALL

Peter Pownall was the last of a succession of Pownalls to occupy this site, their name being given to the surrounding hamlet of Pownall Green. Earlier generations had been Davenport tenants but Peter Pownall's grandfather, William, is thought to have purchased the land and built the hall as he was the first to leave the property in his will. This and his inventory suggest a degree of

POWNALL HALL C1910.

wealth, helped no doubt by his marriage to an heiress. The inventory (2 April 1737) shows the farm having a house (i.e. a living
room), parlour, kitchen, buttery, two chambers (one "the best") and
outbuildings containing tools, cheese, grain, etc. (See appendix
5e).
Ordnance Survey maps (1872 & 1910) show a group of buildings, one of
which we know to have been a cottage, around the farmyard.
Bagshaw's Directory for 1850 describes "an ancient house at Pownall
Green, the residence and property of Peter Pownall Esq." The
Brocklehurst family inherited the farm from Peter Pownall and
immediately sold off all the farm stock and implements, letting the
hall and cottages to a succession of tenants. By 1906 the hall was
occupied by Mr Arthur Lewis Adkinson, a builder. A photograph of
the building taken about 1910 suggests that it had been renovated
since Bagshaw's description.
During the 1914-18 war the farm was run by Land Army girls and the
second world war saw the hall in use as the local food office, and a
German prisoner helping on the farm. The last tenants were the
Gresty family, before the hall was demolished about 1967. One of the
old stone gateposts and the original weeping-ash tree can still be
seen. The Bramhall Moat House Hotel now occupies the site.

POWNALL, MARY (1773-1833)
Peter's sister Mary is mentioned only once in the diary when she began her accounts (**2 February 1784**). (See ACCOMPTS). She never married and, according to Burton, became Peter Pownall's housekeeper and met her death by burning.

POWNALL, PETER (?-1791)
Peter Pownall's father, also Peter, was married twice; first in 1750 to Jane Hulme, who died after child birth in 1752; then in 1759 to Alice **Birch** who bore him seven children, of whom Peter was the third. All were baptised at **Dean Row Chapel**, Wilmslow.

REAR VIEW POWNALL HALL.   c.1960 JK.

POWNALL, PETER; AUTHOR OF THE DIARY (1765-1858)
Peter was born on 13 September and baptised at Dean Row Chapel on 11 October 1765. He died a bachelor at the age of 93 on 3 November 1858 and was buried at **St Mary's Church** Stockport. His diary, including the accounts, covers the years 1782-1808 and was begun when he was just 17.
He seems to have been involved in the running of the farm from an early age. He was the second son and third child of Peter Pownall by his second marriage to Alice née **Birch**. Apart from his birth we have found no further references to the first son John, who may have died in infancy. The rest of the children include Jane (his half sister), Sarah, Alice, William and Mary, who are all mentioned in the diary, and the youngest daughter, Elizabeth Ainsworth.
Peter Pownall, his family and their friends and associates were closely involved with the **Unitarian** Chapel at **Dean Row**. Peter Pownall records payment of pew rents (**29 July 1787**) and in 1800 he was appointed a trustee. In 1851 he served his turn as **overseer for the poor** as had his father before him.
In the 1851 census Peter is described as a "landed proprietor". His will and other documents indicate that as well as being the second largest landowner in Bramhall, with 176 acres, he also owned estates elsewhere in the area. His property included a coal wharf (rail) in Cheadle Bulkeley which he rented to Lord Vernon, who owned coal mines in **Poynton**.
He was both an arable and stock farmer. (See CALVED) He appears to have been a successful business man as well; evidence suggests he lent considerable sums of money. See PRINCIPAL.
On his death Peter Pownall left the greater part of his property to his late sister Sarah's sons, William, John and Thomas **Brocklehurst** of Macclesfield. It was announced in the Stockport Advertiser that the stock, crops and farming equipment at **Pownall Hall** were to be auctioned on 3 December 1858. Pownall Hall Farm was subsequently let and the lands sold at various times. See Appendices 5 & 6a.

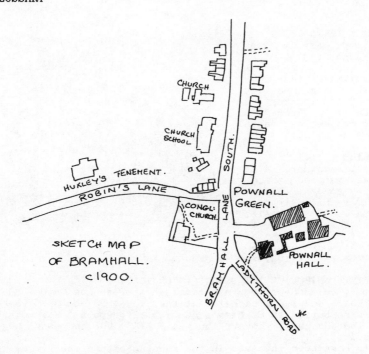

SKETCH MAP
OF BRAMHALL.
c1900.

POWNALL, WILLIAM (?-1736)
Peter Pownall's grandfather, William, married Mary an heiress with lands in High Legh. Between 1716 and 1726 there are many references to him serving as a juror at the Bramhall **Manor Court**. When he died his inventory valued his goods, including cattle, corn, hay and cheese at £403. His Bramhall property passed first to his eldest son John, a bachelor, then to his next son, Peter, father of the diarist. See Appendix 5

POWNALL, WILLIAM (1771-1806)
Peter's younger brother William appears regularly in the diary as he was a boarder at **Stand School** at the time. He never married and died at the age of 35.

POYNTON LAY see LAYS and Appendix 3

POYNTON PARK
The park is on the east side of the Macclesfield road, A523. The hall, family seat of the **Warrens**, was demolished in the mid 19th century, at about the time that the manorial rights and estates were sold. Part of some nearby buildings was developed into a house known as the Towers, which was demolished shortly after the last war. The remains of a lodge and gateway to the Towers can be seen at the end of South Park Drive. In the diary Peter **Pownall** seems to be considering buying cattle from the Warrens. **(23 August 1784)**

PRESBYTERIANS
The Presbyterians were one of the largest **nonconformist** groups in Cheshire during the 17th century. They were sympathetic to the restoration of Charles II but did not benefit from his promise of "a liberty to tender consciences" given in the Declaration of Breda in 1660. Many Anglican clergymen refused to give up their Presbyterian principles at the Restoration, and were consequently ejected from their livings. After a period of harassment, the 1689 Toleration Act allowed Presbyterian ministers and their congregations a measure of freedom of worship (so long as they were licensed by the bishop or the magistrates) but not political or social equality. This led to a recovery in numbers particularly in this area, where there was widespread support. See UNITARIANS

PRESCOTT (PRESCOT), CHARLES (1745-1820)
Rector of Stockport Parish Church from 1783 **(25 May 1784)**. His son, Charles Kenrick Prescot MA, succeeded him. On his death in 1875 the **parish** was divided into two rectories, St Thomas' and **St Mary's**. See DYSON, MISS and PARISH

PRES(T)BURY WAKES see WAKES

PRIESTNALL, MR see CHEESE SELLING

PRINCIPAL
An original or capital sum. In the days before banks people with money to spare frequently lent it to others, to be repaid with interest. Both Peter **Pownall** and his father lent money in this way **(1 January 1783)**. In the accounts for February 1783 Peter Pownall records the interest, at 5%, paid to him on £2,000 by William **Brockle-hurst**. He also lent money to Bramhall **Township**, where in 1832 the accounts of the **over-seer of the poor** show payment of £7 interest on a capital loan of £140.

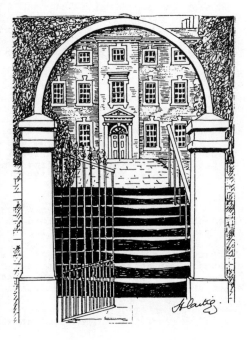

PUSH-PLOUGH see BREAST PLOUGH

THE OLD RECTORY

QUARTER DAYS
These are four days fixed by custom to divide the year into quarters, and were used to determine the dates of tenancies, rents etc. They are Lady Day, 25 March; Midsummer Day, 24 June; Michaelmas, 29 September and Christmas, 25 December.

QUARTER SESSIONS

Quarter sessions were courts held by members of the commission of peace or **justices of the peace**. In most counties of England these were formed in the 14th century. From 1414 the sessions were held four times a year, which probably accounts for their name. **Quarter sessions in Cheshire** started later.

QUARTER SESSIONS IN CHESHIRE

Cheshire was later than other counties in appointing justices outside the county town. It was not until 1536 that the Cheshire equivalent of **quarter sessions** were held regularly. They took place at five different centres: Chester, Knutsford, Middlewich, Nantwich and Northwich. After 1760 only two towns were used: Chester at Epiphany (January) and Easter (April), and **Knutsford** at Midsummer (July) and Michaelmas (October). Cases to be presented were heard at the next sessions, not necessarily the nearest town. Even so some cases took up to two years to be completed. Courts dealt with a variety of cases such as murder, riot, theft, assault, poaching, failure to observe the poor law, **highway** and **bridge maintenance**, **ale houses**, false measure and the sale of substandard goods. In 1888 the Local Government Act transferred the administrative functions of quarter sessions to the county councils. See KNUTSFORD SESSIONS

RABBIT

Rabbits or coneys, as they were formerly called, may have originated in France and were known to the Romans, who preferred to eat the unborn young. They were introduced into England by the 12th century as a source of "live" winter meat and fur, and were kept in warrens. Rabbit stealing was considered a serious offence. Around the 17th century, due to changes in land use and the preservation of game by the control of predators, the rabbit population rapidly increased. During the breeding season from January to August litters may be produces monthly. **(15 October 1782)**

RACES

Peter **Pownall** attended race meetings at Knutsford, Macclesfield, Manchester, Wilmslow and Woodford on a number of occasions, possibly to transact business as well as for the sport, as was the custom. Due to royal support in the reign of Charles II and the breeding of improved racehorses, public interest in horseracing steadily increased. At Knutsford the races were held from at least 1729 and became a very fashionable event. Races had already taken place in Manchester for several centuries before the building of the last race course on Kersal Moor in 1733. The final races took place there in November 1963. The course was sold in 1967 and is now the site of Salford University student village. **(7 October 1783)**

RECOGNIZANCE ROLL

A list of licensed **alehouse** keepers. Each licensee appeared before a **JP** and undertook, with two other people standing surety (usually in the sum of £10), to conduct his alehouse in an orderly manner. See ALE SELLING LICENCE

RECTOR

The rector, or parson, was a priest in full charge of a **parish**. He was entitled to receive **tithes** and other dues from his parishioners. He was said to be the holder of a benefice. In the Middle Ages it became common for the tithes of parishes to be donated to monasteries, who thereby became nominal rectors. The actual services and other parish duties were normally carried out by the monk's **vicar**, from the Latin for representative. After the dissolution of the monasteries (1536-41) these appropriated rectories, as they were called, were frequently sold to laymen, who thus became owners of the tithes.

RECUSANT
One who refused to attend the services of the Church of England, not only Roman Catholics but also **Presbyterians** and Quakers. Puritans were not recusants as such since they normally attended church services, while attempting to alter them and often succeeding.

RELIEF
Aid provided by offertory collections at **parish** churches, alms, charities or **poor lays**. This means of relief varied over the centuries and included **outdoor relief** at home; indoor relief in the **poorhouse** or **workhouse**; care of the sick, the aged, the impotent poor and the insane; boarding out of orphans and the aged; rudimentary schooling and the apprenticeship of children; payment of rent; provision of clothes and medical and midwifery services. See POOR, OVERSEER OF THE

RENNET
Cheese is made by souring the milk and the process can be improved by adding rennet. This was made by soaking the fourth stomach of a suckling calf in strong salt water. The stomach is called a "vell" and can be stored when dry. Rennet is also used to make junket.

RENT
Peter Pownall rented out some land, houses, cottages and farm buildings. Some of his labourers paid rent for their cottages. Many were on Pownall Green and were occupied by families of the same name for years. In 1807 he received £213 8s 0d from rents which were paid twice a year and in 1842 he leased 18 houses and gardens, some of which had crofts and intakes (**inclosed** land). (Accounts 18 December 1782)

RESIDEN(C)E see SETTLEMENT and STRANGER

RICHMOND, MISS
This may refer to either Frances or Anne, who were the daughters of the Rev Richmond, rector of Stockport between 1749-69. The family lived in Millgate Hall, Stockport. (**17 March 1785**). See WORKHOUSE

RIGHT OF COMMON see COMMONER

ROADES, FAMILY
References to the name appear in Bramhall as early as the 17th century. A Thomas Roades, husbandman and tenant farmer, died in 1615; a John Roades is said to have fought for Cromwell, while in 1719 another Thomas Roades was a **juror** and an **affeeror**. In the same

83

year an Edward Roades was a **moorlooker** for Bramhall **Moor**. The
following year a George Roades was accused of harbouring a **stranger**.
During the period of the diary Peter **Pownall** employed two Thomas
Roades, one as a living-in servant and the other, along with a John
and James Roades, as a casual labourer. We have no details as to
why Thomas Roads's goods were sold **(28 October 1782)**. In 1826 a Mr
Roades, **surveyor of the highway** in Bramhall, was ordered to collect
his own **lays**. The 1841 census shows a James Rhodes farming at New
House Farm. He had a considerable household including a coachman
and his family. Bramhall's first postmaster was Peter Rhodes.

ROADS, SIDE OR MINOR
Side roads were the responsibility of those whose land they border-
ed. At the meetings of the Bramhall **manor court** tenants were ordered to carry out maintenance. In 1718 Matthew Chorlton was ordered
to "repair the footeway over against his croft or pay 3s 4d"; the
following year Thomas **Benison**, occupant of George Pattrick Croft to
"repair the Laine over against his croft or pay 13s 4d".

ROBERSON, JONATHAN see SCHOOL, ROBINSON'S

ROTATED CROPS
The rotation of crops was an ancient practice to preserve the fertility of the soil and it was a condition of some Davenport leases in
Bramhall. The crop grown on a field changed each year, for example
barley, then **wheat** and lastly **beans**. The fourth year the ground lay
fallow, and stock might be grazed on it. By the 18th century the
order had become more complicated, for example on some farms the
order was **oats**, fallow, wheat, oats, then the field was sown with
grass and **clover** and used as pasture (see LAYS) for five or six
years before being ploughed up again. **(11 March 1783)**

RYE see BEEHIVES

SADDLE TAX
This tax was introduced in 1761 and lasted until 1875. It was very
unpopular, especially in Stockport where, on 27 November 1784, a
local farmer, Jonathan Thatcher, saddled and bridled his cow and
rode it to market as a protest. A political cartoon recorded the
scene at the foot of Mealhouse Brow, with this verse beneath. "Tax
on Horses shall be void, for on my Cush I mean to ride. Let each
like me strive to outwit, and drown all taxes in a Pitt" (Pitt the
Younger).

SAINTS' DAYS
Some of the better known Saints' days are listed below. Festivals
such as Easter which vary from year to year are omitted.

ALBAN	22 June
ALL SAINTS (ALL HALLOWS)	1 November
ALL SOULS	2 November
ST ANDREW	30 November
ST AUGUSTINE	26 May
ST BARNABAS	11 June
ST BARTHOLOMEW	24 August

CANDLEMAS	2 February
ST CATHERINE OF ALEXANDRIA	25 November
ST CECILIA	22 November
CHILDERMAS (HOLY INNOCENTS' DAY)	28 December
CHRISTMAS	25 December (Quarter day)
ST CHRISTOPHER	25 July
ST CLARE	12 August
ST CLEMENT	23 November
ST COLUMBA	9 June
ST CRISPIN	25 October
ST CUTHBERT	20 March
ST DAVID	1 March
ST DUNSTAN	19 May
ST EDWARD THE CONFESSOR	13 October
ST EDWARD THE MARTYR	18 March
EPIPHANY	6 January
ST ETHELBERT OF KENT	25 February
ST FINAN	17 February
ST FRANCIS OF ASSISI	4 October
ST GEORGE	23 April
HALLOW'EN (ALL HALLOW'S EVE)	31 October
ST HILDA	17 November
ST JAMES THE GREATER	25 July
ST JOAN OF ARC	30 May
NATIVITY OF ST JOHN THE BAPTIST	24 June
ST JOHN THE DIVINE	27 December
ST JOSEPH	19 March
LADY DAY, ANNUNCIATION OF THE BLESSED VIRGIN MARY	25 March (Quarter day)
LAMMAS	1 August
ST LAWRENCE OF CANTERBURY	3 February
ST LUKE	18 October
ST MARGARET OF SCOTLAND	16 November
ST MARK	25 April
MARTINMAS (SAINT MARTIN OF TOURS)	11 November
ASSUMPTION OF ST MARY BLESSED VIRGIN	15 August
ST MARY MAGDALEN	22 July
ST MATTHEW	21 September
ST MATTHIAS	24 February
MICHAELMAS (ST MICHAEL THE ARCHANGEL)	29 September (Quarter day)
MIDSUMMER (NATIVITY OF ST JOHN THE BAPTIST)	24 June (Quarter day)
ST NICHOLAS	6 December
ST OSWALD OF NORTHUMBRIA	9 August
ST PATRICK	17 March
ST PETER AND PAUL	29 June
ST PHILIP AND JAMES THE LESS	1 May
ST SIMON AND JUDE	28 October
ST STEPHEN	26 December
ST SWITHIN	15 July
ST THOMAS	21 December
ST THOMAS OF CANTERBURY	29 December
ST THOMAS MORE	9 July
ST TIMOTHY	24 January
ST VALENTINE	14 February

GLOSSARY

ST VITUS   15 June
ST WILFRID   12 October

SALARY
Payment for a seat or pew.   See DEAN ROW CHAPEL; PEW RENTS

SANDY BROW
An area of land which formed a natural amphitheatre, situated below
the old Stockport Sunday School, near the site of the present roundabout on Piccadilly.   Public meetings were held here and the **militia**
used it for training

SCHOOL, BRAMHALL
The earliest reference we have found is in the Stockport Parish
Register, on 28 March 1588, when William Errwood, son of the
"scholem[as]t[er] of Bramhall was baptised.   In 1643 William Thomson
of Bramhall, "scoolemaister", valued the possessions of Royalist
sympathisers for the Parliamentarians.   The first school building
was said to be a black and white timber framed cottage on **Bramhall
Green**.   A stone plaque recorded "This school was built at the
expense of Warren Davenport clerke [priest] and Esquire in the year
1741." He was lord of the manor at the time.   In 1877 the building
was converted into two cottages which have since been demolished.
(12 April 1784) That year a Board School was opened at Pownall
Green.   Owen records a dame school held by the widow of Charles Leah
in a barn built onto a cottage in Benja Fold which numbered our
Peter Pownall among its pupils.   At the beginning of this century
there was a fee-paying grammar school on the site of the present
library. See METHODISM AND PETER POWNALL

BRAMHALL GREEN.   c 1900

SCHOOL MASTER see SCHOOL, BRAMHALL

SCHOOL, ROBINSON'S
This school was endowed by Jonathan Robinson, a Stockport gentleman, who on his death in February 1792 bequeathed the income (£30 p.a.) from rents of "the Woods", three **Cheshire acres** in Cheadle Hulme which he had previously purchased from John Fallows, to the school. It and school house were built circa 1785 on Schole Croft, the site of the present Cheadle Hulme High School, Woods Lane. It provided free places for four boys and four girls who were taught reading, writing and accounts. The girls were also taught to knit and sew by the schoolmaster's wife (or by an assistant teacher). Among the names of the 15 trustees appears that of Peter **Pownall** (?Snr). The trustees (who met quarterly) selected suitable children for the free places and, when necessary, appointed the master. **(25 January 1787)**

SCORE
Twenty, from the practice of counting sheep in twenties and making a score or mark on a stick for each twenty. **(25 October 1784)**

SET
To plant seeds, young plants, tubers or bulbs. **(14 March 1783)**

SET GEESE see GEESE and GEESE, SET

SETTLEMENT
The 1662 Act of Settlement ruled that any **"stranger"** living in the **parish** or **township** could be removed by the **overseer of the poor** within 40 days unless he rented property worth at least £10 a year. The act provided for settlement certificates for migrant harvesters and in 1697 a further act extended this provision to migrant paupers. The certificates gave a migrant the right to live in a parish or township temporarily, without acquiring legal settlement, but his original parish or township had to support him should he become eligible for **relief**. Since the money for poor relief came from the householders' **poor lays** they were eager to keep the number of dependent poor as low as possible.
Examples of testing for rights of settlement (or residence) appear in the diary **(24 April 1783 & 11 May 1787)**. The court rolls contain several references, for example "We desire our good Master and Landlord William Davenport Esquire that he would presently remove out of this Lordshippe ould Kinsey wife and her Grandchild least the damage of their future maintenance be cast upon himself... (for being poor **strangers)** and not uppon the parish" (Midsummer Court 1650). Also "We ...**emercy Sarah..Roads** to remove Peter Adshead or cause him to bring a certificate to satisfie the Towne" (November Court 1720). In 1808 Thomas Penney claimed relief from Bramhall and was refused. His case was taken to **quarter sessions** at Knutsford where it was proved that his home **parish** was Handforth, and he was returned there. The cost of the action was £20.

SHAW FAMILY
Joseph Shaw served in the **militia** and was demobilised in 1783 **(18 March 1783)**. He **married** Jenny **Glave** three months later. In the census returns for 1841 a Joseph Shaw, aged about 75, was farming on

Kitts **Moss** but his wife is named Martha. His son was an agricultural labourer and his daughter a **silk weaver**. In 1841 Eli Shaw, a
labourer aged about 30, lived with his wife Lucy, also a silk
weaver, at Pownall Green. An Ann Shaw's connections were less
amicable (see KNUTSFORD SESSIONS). In the diary Joshua Shaw rented
lays for his calves from Peter Pownall **(6 January 1783)** and his
death is recorded **(14 October 1785)**.

SHEARING
In Cheshire the word shearing was frequently used for cutting the
corn (7 October 1782), but there are also references to sheep
shearing **(28 June 1784)**.

SHEEP
Peter Pownall does not appear to have had many sheep although he
rented sheep lays to others. He marked his sheep **(15 October 1782)**,
washed sheep **(25 May 1784)** and sheared them **(28 May 1784)**. He also
had three sheep worried, presumably, as today, by stray or uncon-
trolled dogs **(18 February 1784)**. At that time of year the ewes
would have been in lamb and at greatest risk. That year he sold his
lambs **(9 June 1784)**. The next year he sold his ewes as well as lambs
(14 May 1785). He makes no further mention of sheep, nor are any
recorded in his **inventory**.

SHEEP LAYS
Sheep lays were areas of pasture where sheep were grazed during the
winter, fed extra food during spells of severe weather and supervised during lambing. Peter **Pownall** "admitted" sheep into the
winter lay **(10 October 1782 & 9 October 1783)**. There were also
summer lays on higher ground. Some local farmers had lays in the
Macclesfield area and in Derbyshire. See LAY OR LEY

SHEWING see SHOEING

SHIPPEN (SHIPPON)
A cow house or cattle shed. See LAID COWS IN

SHOEING
James **Goulden** was one of the Bramhall **blacksmiths**, and presumably
was employed by the **Pownalls. (15 September 1786)**

SILK WEAVERS
It was common for agricultural families to subsidise their incomes
with other occupations and, in Bramhall, there were many hand-loom
weavers. The looms were set up in any room in their cottages, in
cellars or in custom built extensions (loom shops or sheds). Any
spare loom space could be rented to other weavers. Many were silk
weavers who collected their materials from the silk mills in
Macclesfield, and returned the woven cloth there. They were paid by
the "piece" , usually 60-70 metres in length, which took about a
month to weave. In the 1900s they usually received between £2-£3
per piece according to quality. It is not surprising that the sound
of the shuttle was described as "poverty knocking". There were
groups of weavers living on Bramhall Moor at Grundy Fold (Dorchester
Road today), Mount Pleasant (Hazel Grove), Kitts Moss, Benja Fold,

Pownall Green and Lumb Lane. The **Brocklehursts** are associated with silk manufacture. See BROCKLEHURST, JOHN (1754-1839)

SISTER SARAH see BROCKLEHURST, SARAH

SLIP GOOSEBERRIES
Probably to take cuttings from a bush for propagation. **(22 October 1783)**

SLUCH
A dialect form of the word sludge; the mud, mire or ooze forming a deposit in the bottom of ponds and rivers. **(17 August 1786)**

SMITH
Literally one who hammers metal, from the Old English "smite". There were several different crafts associated with the heating and hammering of metal. The whitesmith and tinsmith worked with "white" metal or tin, the silversmith and goldsmith worked in fine or valuable metals and the **blacksmith** worked with heavy metals like iron.

SOWING
Seed was sown by hand, throwing it broadcast across the ploughed and sometimes **harrowed** soil. It was a skilled occupation requiring an even rhythm or the crops would grow in patches. After sowing the ground was often harrowed to cover the seed and to draw it into furrows. About the time of the diary Jethro Tull invented a drill which enabled the seeds to be sown mechanically. Peter Pownall makes no mention of using new machinery. **(21 November 1782).** See CROSS PLOUGHING

STAND SCHOOL
Stand Grammar School, in north Manchester, was endowed by Henry Siddall in 1688. A single storey school was built by the **Unitarians** next to their Chapel in Whitefield, and a second storey was added at a later date. "Twenty young gentlemen" scholars paid four guineas (£4 4s) a term to be taught "English, Geography, Writing and **Accompts**." Peter **Pownall's** young brother, William, was a pupil at the school from August 1784 (aged 13 years) until 1788. By the 19th century the school had 85 pupils. In 1913 a new building was erected a mile away. **(16 August 1784).** See MANCHESTER ACADEMY

STAVED
Describes vessels made from strips of wood (staves) such as barrels, tubs and casks. This is an ancient craft, for barrels are mentioned in the Old Testament.

STINT see COMMON OF PASTURE

STIRK
A cow or bull between one and two years old. **(11 October 1784)**

ST MARY'S CHURCH
St Mary's is the **parish** church of Stockport and stands at the south end of the marketplace. The earliest records show a church on the

OLD ST MARY'S CHURCH.

site by 1334. The bell tower was built about 1616 and demolished in 1810. The church was rebuilt, apart from the 14th century chancel, between 1813 and 1817 and reconsecrated the following year. Peter Pownall mentions the old church. He and his family are buried in the graveyard. **(10 September 1787).** See appendix 5d

STOCKPORT ASSEMBLY
We have not been able to trace where the Stockport assembly was held. It would have been a social gathering similar to a dance. Assemblies were very popular among the gentry in the 18th century and are described by Jane Austen in Northanger Abbey. **(3 February 1787)**

STOCKPORT CHAPEL
Possibly the **Presbyterian** chapel built in 1721, which once stood in High Street. Sometime later it became the first Stockport Meeting House for the **Unitarians**. Among those buried in the graveyard are members of the **Benison** and **Marsland** families. A new Unitarian chapel was built in 1841, in Petersgate. **(11 February 1787)**

STOCKPORT FAIR see FAIR, STOCKPORT

STOCKPORT ILLUMINATED
George III was subject to bouts of "madness". It is now thought that he was suffering from porphyria, the symptoms of which are severe pain and sensitivity to light. His first attack occurred in 1788 and his subsequent recovery was celebrated nationally, not least by Stockport. **(20 March 1789)**

STOCKPORT MARKET see MARKET, STOCKPORT

STOCKPORT OLD CHURCH see ST MARY'S CHURCH

STOCKS
The Bramhall stocks, or a replica, now stand in the courtyard of **Bramall Hall**. They used to be on **Bramhall Green**. The person being punished sat on a bench with his wrists or ankles pinioned between two wooden bars. Stockport had a pillory in the **market** place, a similar framework set on a post so that the person had to stand, with his head and wrists imprisoned. Part of the punishment was being thus exposed to public ridicule but unpopular prisoners were also shied with unpleasant missiles.

STORE PIGS see PIGS

STRANGER
One living in the manor without **settlement**. See COURT ROLLS; SOME COMMONLY USED WORDS, stranger

STRAW
Straw is the stalks of **wheat, oats, barley** or **rye** left after **threshing**. It has a variety of uses including animal bedding, which can be used afterwards as manure; cattle **fodder** (wheat and rye straw); thatching and making **beehives** (rye is preferred); making rope, baskets, mats, whole chairs and seats of chairs and stools. According to his accounts Peter **Pownall** sold his straw to many of the customers who purchased his **hay**, presumably as bedding. One regular customer was a Mr Fidler, who may have been one of the Fidler family who were landlords of the Red Lion, **Bullock Smithy**, from 1754. It was a staging post for the London coaches and had extensive stabling. (Accounts 13 June 1805)

STRIKES
We do not know what Peter **Pownall** intended to use the iron for. It may be a form of the word "strake". **(26 March 1785)**. See WHEELWRIGHT and WEIGHTS AND MEASURES

ST SWITHENS see OLD SWITHEN'S DAY and SAINTS' DAYS

STUBBLE
The stalks of grain left sticking up after harvest. Peter **Pownall** was ploughing a field where grain had been grown the previous year. **(11 March 1783)**

STUBBLE GOOSE see GEESE

STUBLE see STUBBLE

SUBSIDY ROLLS
These are records of subsidies granted to the crown from the 13th century to 1689 in the form of taxes. They are in the Public Record Office, London, and give details of the payers of taxes such as poll tax (personal tax) and **hearth tax**.

SUIT AND SERVICE
Bramhall leases included suit and service. The former was the obligation of the tenant to attend his lord's court; the latter included customary duties such as **boonwork**, hedging and ditching, **highway maintenance**, the grinding of all grains at the lord's **mill** and payment of a **heriot** on the death of a tenant. Military service was included in the 17th century leases.

SUMMER WORK
Ground which had lain **fallow** was ploughed during the summer ready for autumn sowing. **(10 June 1783)**

SUMMONS see POOR, OVERSEER OF THE

SURVEYOR OF THE HIGHWAY see HIGHWAY, OVERSEERS OF THE

SWEDES see TURNIPS

TAXES
Peter **Pownall** paid many taxes to the government. According to his accounts in 1808 these included half yearly payments of dog tax 10s; **horse tax** - riding horses £4 and draught horses 18s 9d; tax on male servants £1 15s; house tax 10s 8d and **window tax** £4 12s 6d. (The latter is a very large sum and may include other houses as well as Pownall Hall). He also paid income tax, which was first levied in 1799, at 2s in the £1 to pay for the war with France. It was abolished in 1802 but only for one year. In 1807 Peter Pownall's income tax was £2 10s. See CART TAX; HEARTH TAX and SADDLE TAX

TEA SET
(HANDLELESS CUP)   C 1775.

TEA
Tea drinking started in England in the mid 1600s. At first it was taken by the ladies after dinner, when they left the gentlemen to their wine and tobacco. Later it was fashionable as an accompaniment to conversation. All tea was very expensive due to the high taxes so the lady of the house kept it locked in an elegant caddy. China

tea was more commonly used as Indian tea was the more expensive and considered a delicacy. The tea making ceremony was elaborate; heated water was brought by the maid, and sometimes reheated by the hostess in a kettle over a spirit stove or "Indian Furnace", and the tea was made at the table. The tea pot was of porcelain or silver, often with a stand and the tea was served in small handleless cups on saucers. If sweetmeats or tiny cakes were offered they were held in the fingers until eaten. Peter **Pownall's** family often took tea with their friends. **(14 November 1782)** In his accounts for January 1807 he paid £3 18s 9d to **Mr Brocklehurst** for "tea, cocoa, etc." and in March the same year £3 13s for tea alone. Tea leaves were often dried and re-used for the servants' tea, and damp tea leaves were sprinkled on the floors to lay the dust when sweeping.

THATCHED BEEHIVES see BEEHIVES

THRASHING see THRESHING

THRAVE
A measure of sheaves (a sheaf is a bundle of stalks of corn tied together), usually 12 or can be 24 sheaves of corn. Mentioned in Appendix 5b

THRESHING
The threshing of **corn** was carried out throughout the year as grain was required. The sheaves of corn were loosened and spread on a winnowing sheet of heavy canvas on the threshing floor of the barn. Then the men took flails and beat at the corn until the hard grain fell from the ears. The grain was cleaned or winnowed by tossing it from sieves into the air so that the draught would blow the chaff off. The grain was then ready for the **mill**. The **straw** and chaff could be used as **fodder**. Although threshing machines were invented in 1636 the first patented machine did not appear until 1788. During the next hundred years the designs improved and contractors hauled their machines from farm to farm. We do not know whether machines were used on the **Pownall** farm but small quantities of corn continued to be threshed by hand for many years. **(24 March 1783)**

TIMBER
Peter **Pownall** had an estate in Mottram St Andrew from which he sold £210 worth of timber but he waited over a year for the full payment **(21 March 1786)**. As Bagshaws directory of 1805 lists the Misses Massey as tanners of Mottram St Andrew, it is possible that Edmund and Daniel Massey were members of that family and were buying the timber to use the bark for tanning **(2 January 1787)**. In the accounts there are two further references to timber, one for a sale of £3 15s 4d worth (15 May 1807) and payment to John Brown of 8s 2d for "Taking a Tree to Stockport" (4 May 1807).

TITHE
The tithe was a tenth part of the annual produce of agriculture or labour, being a tax payable in kind for the support of the parish priest and the church. Originally there were two kinds of tithe. The "great" (predial or rectorial) tithe was composed of the most valuable and easily collected produce such as **corn**, **hay**, wood and

fruit and was paid to the **rector**. The "small" (mixed or vicarial) tithe was the rest, such as milk, live animals, garden and artisan products, less valuable and more difficult to handle, which was frequently given to the **vicar** as his income. The incumbent had to pay for the upkeep of the chancel fabric but the congregation was responsible for the nave. **(8 August 1783)**

TITHE DAY see TITHES, COLLECTION OF

TITHE MAP
These were maps produced mainly between 1838 and 1854 because of the 1836 Tithe Act and show fields, their acreage and produce; crofts and gardens; and owners and tenants. See TITHES, COMMUTATION OF

TITHES, COLLECTION OF
Quite often the arduous task of collecting the tithes in kind was carried out by a **farmer**. This practice continued after commutation (see below) as James **Goulden** was farmer in 1783. He held a meeting at the Dog and Partridge Inn, Bramhall (now Great Moor) when payments were made. This may have been quite a social occasion. **(8 August 1783)**.

TITHES, COMMUTATION OF
The difficulty of collecting and storing the produce led to the use of money payments in lieu (commutation). By 1780 this had become common practice. With the 1836 Tithe Act dues became a **corn** rent, which was a variable payment, reviewed every seven years and adjusted to the average market price of corn. The 1925 Tithe Act abolished the rent charges. In 1936 the Tithe Act ended all tithe payments but created Government stocks called Tithe Redemption Annuities (Queen Anne's Bounty) which were given in compensation.

TOWNSHIP
In areas where **parishes** were too large for competent administration they were divided into smaller units or townships. Around here, in northeast Cheshire, a township was co-extensive with a manor, and the **manor court** looked after most of the township's affairs.

TREFOIL
A plant of the pea-flower family, grown with **clover** to make **hay**. **(25 April 1787)**

TURBARY
The householders' right to cut peat (or turf) on **waste** land from a specified area or **moss room**. The **manor court** controlled this right. In 1645 Richard Berchenshaw was presented for "taking away turves out of a room belonging to Seeles tenement". See MOSSES OR MOORS

TURKEY
Judging by how often Peter **Pownall** sent turkeys to his friends it seems likely that he bred them. The earliest reference we have found to turkey flesh being used as food is in 1573. They were said to have been brought to Europe by the Spanish from Mexico in the 16th century. **(4 December 1782)**

TURNIPS
Turnips were a new crop in the 18th century and were not generally grown in this area until 1840. Peter Pownall, however, was growing them in 1786 which is further evidence of his advanced ideas **(3 July 1786)**. Yellow turnips may have been swedes, originally known as Swedish turnips **(25 April 1787)**. They were grown as winter **fodder** for cattle. Nowadays the feeding of turnips to milking cows is thought to taint the milk, so they are given after milking to lessen this risk.

TWINTER
A beast two winters old. **(12 May 1784)**

UNITARIANS
The first Unitarian church was opened by Theophilus Lindsey in London in 1774. The form of service depended on the wishes of the minister and his congregation. Marriage and christening ceremonies could take the traditional form but variations were common. The beliefs of the church are signified in its name, the aim for a sense of "one-ness", and God is conceived as one person in contrast to the Trinity of orthodox Christianity. It was the clause relating to the Trinity in the Act of Toleration 1689 which excluded the Unitarians from political office. See DEAN ROW CHAPEL; PRESBYTERIANS; MANCHESTER ACADEMY and STAND SCHOOL

VEGETABLES
In the 18th century there was an increase in the proportion of vegetables in the diet. Gilbert White, writing in 1778, referred to all levels of the population eating beans, peas and greens. See MARKET GARDENING

VESTRY see PARISH VESTRY

VETCHES
Plants of the pea-flower family. **Rye** grass was often sown with vetch to "hold it up" because of its naturally sprawling form which made it difficult to mow. Unlike **hay**, which was dried, it could be fed green to the cattle. **(24 January 1786)**

VICAR
Where the **tithes** of a parish had been appropriated by an absentee **rector** or lay person, a vicar was appointed to fulfil the duties of the rector. He often received the small tithes for his living.

WAGES
Although the accounts in the diary are not complete it is possible to obtain some idea of the wages paid by Peter **Pownall**. The lowest wages were paid to the boys. Thomas Bayley was paid one shilling a week **(19 April 1784)**. William Bayley received 7 guineas for a year's work, actually eleven months, approximately three shillings a week **(3 January 1785)**. Despite free board and lodging the rates were comparatively low. Twenty years later the farmers' boys were receiving between £2 - £3 10s for 51 weeks work. In 1806 and 1807 Betty, Sarah and James Waters were each receiving nearly £9 a year. The major part of their wages was paid in a lump sum just after

Martinmas but small advances were paid during the year. The men were paid intermittently, presumably according to the work they did, the higher sums being paid during the harvest. A few entries give rates: payment for eight days' mowing was 2s a day, **shearing** was paid at £1 an acre or nine and a half days at 12s. Peter Pownall's rates are considerably lower than those described by Geoffrey Scard for Cheshire farm workers of the period; his rates include £25 per year for a live-in male worker and £14 - £16 for females, while casual Irish labourers were paid 15s-16s a week during harvest.

WAINED COLT
Possibly weaning a colt, teaching the young animal to feed without its mother's milk. Alternatively a "wain" is a four-wheeled open waggon pulled by horses or oxen, and he may have been training the colt as a draught horse. **(5 October 1786)**

WAKES
Wakes were **parish** celebrations held either on the day the church was consecrated or on the **saint's day** to whom it was dedicated. Originally the parishioners fasted and stayed awake all night on the eve of the saint's day, but after the Reformation (Edward VI) the religious aspect declined and the wakes became an excuse for feasting and merrymaking. In 1658 John Morgan, a churchwarden of Cheadle, was accused of "hyreing" his bull to be "baited from **Alehouse** to Alehouse on Cheadle Wakeday". The celebrations died out nationally during the mid 19th century but continued in the northwest as annual holidays. The wake was also the overnight vigil by the body of a deceased knight or other respected person. See BULL BAITING and FAIRS

WAKES, NORBURY
The Norbury Wakes later became the **Bullock Smithy** wakes because part of the old township of Norbury was in the the growing village of Bullock Smithy. The wakes were held on the Sunday nearest to 12th August and during the following week. People travelled from afar to join in the celebrations. Music was provided by the village band, hurdy-gurdy players and itinerant musicians, including "a fiddler in every tap room". Along the streets were stalls filled with sweetmeats, fancy goods and toys, all lit at night by flaring kerosene lamps. During the day there were races and competitions, including jack-ass races of a mile for a £50 prize and sack races for 50s. There were smoking matches, duck swimming, wheelbarrow races and **bull**- and **bear-baiting** according to a poster for 1810. A fair was held on the ground behind the Grove Inn and there was dancing in the streets and **ale houses**. **(23 August 1783)**

WAKES, WILMSLOW
The Wilmslow wakes commemorated the feast of St Bartholomew (Old Calendar) and were held for one week at the beginning of September. The Wilmslow **races** were run the same week and the whole town celebrated the holiday with enthusiasm. There were booths and stalls on the race course, and itinerant entertainers from conjurors to card sharps attended. There was music and step dancing in the taverns every night and much feasting, drinking and rowdiness. **(3 September 1786)**

WALL TREES
Probably the espalier fruit trees which are trained along horizontal wires. Espalier actually means a "fruit wall" and is the lattice framework on which the trees are supported. **(3 February 1783)**

WASHED SHEEP
Sheep are washed or dipped to clean the fleeces before **shearing** and to discourage parasites like ticks and lice. **(25 May 1784)**

WASTE
Land which was not suitable for intensive agriculture was known as waste. In Bramhall this included the boggy, peaty areas known as **moors** or **mosses**, oddments of poor land like Rushy Riddings near Jackson's Lane (described as waste in 1654), and strips of land alongside the roadways. Tenants were allowed to make use of waste land to graze cattle, cut **peat** and dig **marl**. The use was controlled by **moorlookers** appointed by the **manor court**. See COMMON LAND and COMMON OF PASTURE

WATSON, REV MR JOHN
The Rev John Watson, MA, FAS, was presented to **St Mary's** by Sir John Warren in 1769. His death at the age of 59 was noted by Peter **Pownall** in his diary. **(17 January & 14 March 1783)**

WEDDING CLOTHES
In the country districts, in the late 18th century, the bride and groom would have worn their "best" clothes to their wedding. A contemporary example of a wedding dress (1770-85) can be seen in the Gallery of Costume, Platt Hall, Manchester. The dress of red corded silk has a front opening but no form of fastening, it is thought that it was pinned to the stays (stiff corsets) beneath and the join covered by a frilled strip of matching material. On special occasions an embroidered collar and apron was worn. Poorer people wore cotton or printed linen. White wedding dresses were becoming fashionable but were embroidered with coloured flowers. Yellow and blue were also popular for weddings. The bride's hair was often worn loose and garlanded with flowers. The wedding veil and pure white dress appeared in the 19th century. Peter **Pownall's sister Sarah** went to Manchester to buy her wedding clothes only three weeks before her wedding. **(5 March 1783).** See MARRIED

RED SILK WEDDING DRESS 1770-85.

WEIGHTS AND MEASURES
The weights and measures used by Peter Pownall's generation of farmers were very different from today's. A load of **hay** was 36 trusses which weighed 56lb. The most frequently quoted measure is the bushel. This was a measure of capacity, officially four pecks or eight gallons. The com-

modity to be measured was poured into the appropriate container (often **staved)** and a stick or "strike" was drawn across the top to strike off excess measure. The Imperial bushel was 2218.2 cubic inches. The Winchester bushel was 2150.4 cubic inches. The measure varied in weight according to the product. Some examples of variations in the bushel shown below were given by Henry Holland in 1813:

Barley	60 lbs or 38 quarts
Malt	32-36 quarts
Oats	45-50 lbs
Potatoes	90 lbs
Wheat	70-75 lbs

A hundredweight is 112 lbs. A "long hundred" was 120 lbs given to ensure against short measure.

WHEAT
Peter **Pownall** grew only a small amount of wheat as did many other Cheshire farmers. In 1842 it formed less than one fifth of his tot-al **corn** crop, **barley** a fourth and **oats** nearly half. He grew winter wheat which was usually sown in October and November. The summers in this area are too short to ripen spring-sown wheat. Wheat was re-garded as a cash crop, grown for sale to raise money, not nec-essarily for family consumption. **(4 October 1782)**

WHEELWRIGHT
The wheelwright made and repaired wheels for waggons and **carts**. Many were also waggon builders. This was a highly skilled craft and the products lasted for many years. Local **inventories** show pairs of wheels, and parts such as naves (wheel hubs or centres), spokes, felloes (segments of the wooden rims) and strakes (separate curved strips of iron sometimes used instead of an iron hoop tyre). The wheelwright worked with a variety of woods, each selected for its properties. A single wheel may include elm for the nave, oak for the spokes, and ash or beech for the felloes. At the final stage of manufacture the **blacksmith** fitted an iron tyre which was put on while it was red hot, and rapidly cooled with buckets of cold water so that it contracted to fit the wheel tightly.

WHINTERERS see WINTERER

WILL
A legal document drawn up to show how a testator wishes his property to be distributed after his death. Often known as a "will and test-ament", the will refers to the real estate and the testament to personal belongings. See Appendices 5e, 5f & 5g.

WILMSLOW WAKES see WAKES, WILMSLOW

WINDOW TAX
This tax was imposed by Parliament to replace **hearth tax**, and the proceeds were put towards the re-minting of the coinage. After 1792 houses with 7-9 windows were rated at 4s per annum and 10-19 windows at 8s per annum. From 1825 only houses with eight or more were liable. The tax was abolished in 1851. Bricked up windows, to avoid the tax, can still be seen in houses of this period. See TAXES

WINTERER
A beast one winter old. **(7 April 1783)**

WINTER FEED
In the past when grass stopped growing during the winter, farmers had difficulty in finding enough food for their stock. The dairy herds therefore produced no milk. Originally hay, cut from the **meadows**, and **straw** were the main foods used but by the 18th century various methods of increasing winter feed had been introduced. Peter **Pownall** grew **clover**, **trefoils** and **vetches**. Grass from his meadow land was supplemented with more from **lays**. He also grew swedes, **turnips** and cabbages, which could be fed to the dairy herd to extend the milking period. The demand for milk had increased with the growth of nearby industrial towns.

WITFORD
The neighbouring village of Woodford.

WOMAN'S CROFT BRIDGE see BRIDGE, WOMAN'S CROFT and Appendix 4

WOODCOCK
The woodcock is a well camouflaged woodland bird which sits quietly in the undergrowth by day. At dusk it flies to marshy spots and probes in the ground with its long bill for earthworms and insects. Its eyes are set high in its head for all round vision while feeding. During the breeding season it will "rode" (perform a regular circling flight) in the evening. It is still regarded as a **game** bird (Wildlife and Country Act 1971) and the closed season is from 1 February - 30 September. **(9 November 1782)**

WORKHOUSE
Provisions for housing the poor had been made by the Elizabethan Poor Laws. Subsequent acts had encouraged the building of larger institutions and from 1782-3 small **parishes** were allowed to form unions and share the expenses of a workhouse. Records at the Cheshire County Record Office (P10/13/15-26) show references to a Bramhall workhouse, which seems to have been run in co-operation with Handforth-cum-Bosden. The **overseers of the poor's** accounts for 1821 show a payment of £145 11s 1d as half the sum for a Millgate Hall. There were two Millgate Halls in Stockport, one, mentioned in 1577, which became the town-house of the **Warrens** and whose occupancy can be traced until the end of the 19th century. Opposite was the other hall, formerly the town-house of the Bamfords and also marked as Millgate Hall on the Fairbank plans of 1763. This was a workhouse at one time. There are also references to a **poor house**. A Stockport workhouse was built in 1812 on Daw Bank and in 1841 a new one was built to replace it at Shaw Heath, now St Thomas's Hospital. Ideally a workhouse was a place where food, shelter and work were provided for those in need, but in order to discourage scroungers it was thought necessary to make it unattractive. Men and women were separated and their children were housed in a third department, with a school. The work provided was of a repetitive and unpleasant nature. Stockport workhouse had a stone-breaking yard. Local people dreaded the workhouse and many starved rather than enter it. At times of high unemployment the system could not

cope with the enormous numbers seeking relief and so **outdoor relief** had to be provided. Gradually the workhouse became a home for the aged and sick and by 1870 was adopting the role of a hospital. Officially it was not until the 1944 Health Act that workhouses were abolished, although by this time all of them had been hospitals for many years. See POOR, ACCOUNTS OF THE OVERSEER OF THE

WORTHINGTON FAMILY
There were several branches of this family in north Cheshire. In 1666-7 a Martha Worthington married Hugh Pownall, a tanner of Styal. In 1694 Alice, the widow of Hugh Worthington of Styal bequeathed money to Elizabeth, daughter of William **Davenport** (VII) of Bramall Hall. The family had strong **Unitarian** connections; father and son, both Hugh Worthington, were consecutive ministers at **Dean Row Chapel** in the early 18th century. The latter moved to Hale Chapel but was buried at Dean Row in 1773. By 1800 several members of the family were trustees at Dean Row, including Thomas Worthington, tanner of Styal, who may have been Peter **Pownall's** companion on the visit to Liverpool **(15 & 17 May 1787)**. In the diary there are three references to a George Worthington: he went to London **(18 October 1782)**, accompanied Peter Pownall to buy land **(7 March 1785)** and married **(1 February 1786)**. The families met socially; Alice, Peter Pownall's sister, attended the **Stockport Assembly** with the family **(12 January 1783, 3 February & 3 March 1787)**, and a **turkey** was sent to the Worthingtons in December 1782. Regular entries in the accounts show a Mr Worthington buying **oats** (1790-1809). Peter Pownall records the payment of several bills to Mr Worthington for varying amounts between £6-£8 **(1 & 19 January 1787**, Accounts 1806-1808). At this time Hugo Worthington was a solicitor in Altrincham in the house which became the Stamford Estates Office and is now owned by the National Trust. Possibly he was the Pownalls' solicitor. Local references to the name include Samuel Worthington of Chip Hill (1842), George Worthington who appears there in 1883, and John Worthington who with John Smith sold Pepper Street Farm to Peter Pownall in 1843. John Worthington, "tenant" appears in Peter Pownall's will, 1857. See Appendix 5c.

YELLOW TURNIPS see TURNIPS

APPENDICES TO THE GLOSSARY

APPENDIX 1

THE ACCOUNTS WRITTEN OVER DIARY PAGE 44

```
                Bacon        2    8
                Cash         3    -
                Coal              7 1/2
                Meal         5    3
                            ———————————
                            11    6 1/2

                Cash        10    6
   Aug 10th Do              10    -
                Pot'oes      5    4
                Meal         5    0
                Coals        1   10 1/2
                           ————————————
                        1   12    8 1/2
                ?[illeg]     2    3 1/2

   Aug 10       1   15    0

                Wheat        6    6
                Cash         3    -
                Coal              7 1/2
                Cash     1   1    0
                Do           6    0
                           ————————————
                ?[illeg]          8 1/2

                        1   17    9 1/2
                Cash              7 1/2
                           ————————————
                        1   18    5
                             6    7
                           ————————————
                        2    5    0      May 4th
```

TWO PAGES FROM THE ACCOUNTS SECTION OF THE DIARY

Page 86

1807	Recd	£	s	d
Jany 1	Peter Lomas 1/2 yrs Rent due) Michaelmas last)	3	0	0
4	John Gleave 1/2 yrs Rent due) Michaelmas last)	12	10	0

		£	s	d	
	Do a yrs Rent of a croft due)	2	2	0	
	Christmas Day last)				
8	Joshua Murral for besoms [brushes]	0	3	0	
	Do for Pottatoe G[roun]d	0	18	0	
	Mr Brocklehurst for Oats & Stores	8	17	0	
	Do for a yrs Int[erest] of £120 due				
	Nov last	5	12	6	
	Mr Dodge	1	19	0	1/2
	Do	1	19	5	
	Do	1	9	9	
	Do	2	5	9	
16	John Goulden 1/2 yrs Rent due	40	0	0	
	Mr Dodge	1	10	8	
	Do	2	4	6	
22	Hannah Seel for Meal & Flower	21	18	0	
	Saml Shaw for Meal	1	0	0	
30	Mr Dodge	3	11	9	

Page 87

1807	Paid	£	s	d
Jany 1	Settled with James Adsead & paid			
	him his wages in July for 51 Week			
	service ending this Day	2	0	0
1	Settled with Edward Cooper)			
	& paid him his Wages in full for)			
	51 Week service ending this day)		7	6
3	Mr Norths bill	2	13	3
4	Mrs Garner Bull Money		4	0
	[?Stud fees]			
	Mr [?] Hallworth Do		8	0
	Jno Gleave for Beef	16	6	0
8	Joshua Murrall for shear[in]g of corn	0	18	0
	Do for weed[in]g Pottatoes		1	6
	Mr Brocklehurst for Tea Cocoa etc	3	18	9
13	Jas Jarvis for Mr Pickfor for			
	Grinding etc	1	16	0
16	Jno Goulden for Cheese	5	15	0
16	Jno Goulden Income Tax	3	5	0
	Edward Bennet for Beef	0	6	6
22	Mr Washingtons bill	30	13	10
30	Mr Norbury for Malt	13	14	0

A full transcription of all the accounts in the diary has been
deposited at Stockport Library and the University of Reading

APPENDIX 2

RECORD OF CASUAL LABOURERS from 1 JULY 1797

Peter Pownall kept a list of labourers (who helped with the harvest) for July and August from 1796 to 1812 inclusive. Some, like John Brown, rented their cottages from the Pownalls.

Thursday	Samual Brown			one day

Friday	Samual Brown	James Brown		one day

Saturday	Samual Brown James Brown Joseph Brown Thos Leah half day			one day

Monday	Samuel Brown James Brown) Joseph Brown Thomas Leah) Benjamen Goulbern John Brown)			one day

Tuesday	Saml Brown Jas Brown Joseph Brown) Thos Leah Benjamin Golbern John Brown)			one day

Wednesday	Sam Brown Jas Brown Joseph Brown) Thomas Leah Benj Goulbern John Brown)			one day

Thursday	Saml Brown Jas Brown Joseph Brown) John Brown Thos Leah Benjamin Goulbern)			one day

Friday	Saml Brown Jas Brown Joseph Brown) John Brown Benjamin Golbern Thos Leah)			one day

Saturday	Sam Brown Jas Brown Jos Brown) John Brown Benm Golbern Thos Leah)			one day

Monday	Saml Brown Jos Brown Jas Brown) John Brown Benjn Golbern) Thos Leah half day			one day

Tuesday	Saml Brown Jos Brown Jas Brown John Brown Thos Leah - half day			one day

Wednesday	Saml Brown Josp Brown Jas Brown) John Brown Thos Leah Benjamin Golbern)			one day

Thursday	Saml Brown Joseph Brown Jas Brown) John Brown Benjamin Golbern)			one day

Taken   from Pages 66 & 67 of the Diary.   A full   transcription   has been deposited at Stockport Library and the University of Reading.

APPENDIX 3

POYNTON PARK LAYS

From the 10th of May 1788 to the 12 October
At the following prices

	£	s
For one year old colt	1	10
Two year old colt	2	0
Aged horses	2	10
For a calf	0	15
Stirk	1	5
Heifer	1	0
An aged cow	2	5
Milch cow	2	0

Cattle are not to be exchanged after they are taken into the Park, unless they happen to have an accident, or die, when the Owners must sustain the loss, but may replace them by others of the same age. No cattle are to continue in the Lay after the 10th October, and they will not be delivered without payment, neither will any be accepted for this ley after 31 March.

Apply to Mr Brand or Mr Boardman at Stockport, or to Mr Henry Ridgway or to the Herdsman at Poynton.

Taken from the MANCHESTER MERCURY dated Tuesday 18 March 1788

APPENDIX 4

WOMANSCROFT BRIDGE

"Concerning repairs to Bramhall Bridge."

"To his Ma[jes]ty's Justices holding the next Quarter Sessions.

Gentlemen, Wee haveing this day viewed Bramhall Bridge and find it to be much out of repaire and likely in short time to be worse if not timely repaired; it being the first time since it was erected, which we find above 20 years ago. Wee therefore upon complaint to us made thought fit to inform you that the repaireing of this Bridge is very needfull, it being then very servicable to the Countey, but now very dangerous to passengers if the river Brame, on which it stands exceeded its natural boundes. And by our owne Judgment as well as that of some experienced workmen now pr[e]sent Wee believe the sum of £13 6s 8d will repair the same and not under. Mr Davenport of Bramhall p[ro]mising to oversee the work and have the money laid out to best advantage. etc etc

Your humble Servants
Rob[ert] Dukinfield, Edw[ard] Thornycroft
Bramhall 21 March 1699/00
£13 6s 8d W[illia]m Davenport of Bramhall Esq Treas[ure]r."

Ref: <u>The Record Society of Lancashire and Cheshire 1559-1760</u>
<u>Quarter Sessions Records</u> p199 F1 D71 S Chester 12 April 1700

APPENDIX 5

DOCUMENTS RELATING TO PETER POWNALL AND HIS FAMILY

Appendix 5a

THE DEATH OF PETER POWNALL (Author of the diary)

5 November 1858

On the 3rd instant at Pownall Green Bramhall, at the advanced age of 94 years, Mr Peter Pownall

Ref Stockport Advertiser

Appendix 5b

NOTICE OF THE SALE OF THE LATE PETER POWNALL'S STOCK

26 November 1858

Messrs Lucas are honoured with instructions from the executors of the late Peter Pownall Esq to SELL BY AUCTION, on Wednesday next, the 1st day of December, at his late residence, Pownall Green, Bramhall, near Stockport, the Entire STOCK of valuable YOUNG DAIRY COWS, HEIFERS, YOUNG CATTLE, HORSES, HAY, CORN, POTATOES, MANGOLDS, TURNIPS, FARMING IMPLEMENTS, etc comprising 20 first class dairy cows, selected with great care and judgement by their late owner, whose superior knowledge of cattle was proverbial; handsome young bull, two in-calf heifers, one stirk, pair of powerful grey horses; very useful grey horse six years old; brown ditto 6 years old; together with a powerful team; large quantity of hay in sheds, bays, and stacks; 350 thraves of wheat, 700 thraves of oats, 60 tons of mangolds, 30 tons of Swede turnips, 50 loads of potatoes; three broad-wheeled carts with complete fittings; 4 1/2 inch wheeled ditto, iron ploughs, drill and seed harrows, ox harrow, chain and shaft gearing for four horses, land roller, winnowing machine, straw cutter, turnip cutter, ladders, wheel barrows, cart ropes & sheets and a large assortment of smaller implements.

NB Luncheon will be provided at 11 o'clock & the Sale will commence punctually at 12. The Auctioneers respectfully solicit the attention of their friends to this important sale, assuring them that such stock is very rarely offered for public competition. Catalogues may be had on and after the 27th inst, on application to the Auctioneers, at their offices, 26 Great King Street, Macclesfield.

Ref Stockport Advertiser

Appendix 5c

THE WILL OF PETER POWNALL (Author of the diary)

THIS IS THE LAST WILL AND TESTAMENT of me PETER POWNALL of Bramhall
in the County of Chester Esquire made this twenty seventh day of
April in the year of our Lord one thousand eight hundred and fifty
seven FIRST I will and order and direct my Executors hereinafter
named to pay and discharge All my just debts and funeral and testamentary expenses out of my personal estate as soon as conveniently
may be after my death AND I give and devise unto my Nephew William
Brocklehurst of Tytherington in the said County Solicitor and Banker
ALL my Messuages Cottages and tenements with the lands hereditaments
and appurtenances thereunto respectively belonging and chief rents
situate lying and being in Bramhall aforesaid in the occupation of
myself and tenants AND ALSO ALL that my messuage and tenement with
the lands hereditaments and appurtenances thereunto belonging situate lying and being in Mottram [St] Andrew in the said County now
occupied by John Fisher as tenant thereof To hold the same to the
said William Brocklehurst his heirs and assigns for ever AND I give
and Devise unto my nephew John Brocklehurst of Hurdsfield in the
said County Silk Manufacturer and Banker ALL that my messuage and
tenement with the lands hereditaments and appurtenances therunto
belonging situate lying and being in Cheadle Bulkley in the Parish
of Cheadle in the said County known by the name of Cheadle Heath End
now in the occupation of Isaac Higginbotham as tenant thereof AND
also all that yearly chief rent of six pounds twelve shillings and
sixpence payable by Robert Grundy for a plot of land part of Cheadle
Heath End Estate And also all these five several chief rents amount-
ing together to the sum of Seventeen pounds and seven shillings
issuing and payable from a Close of Land lying and being in the
Borough of Stockport in the said County of Chester called Heap
Ridding Meadow AND all those my messuages and tenements with the
lands hereditaments and appurtenances thereunto respectively belonging situate lying and being in Handforth cum Bosden in the said
County now in the several occupations of John Worthington William
Taylor and Thomas Hallworth as tenants thereof AND also all those
two yearly chief rents of two pounds eight shillings and four pence
and Three pounds six shillings and eightpence issuing and payable
from land in Handforth cum Bosden aforesaid which I lately leased to
Thomas Hallworth and Robert Webb To Hold the same to the said John
Brocklehurst his heirs and assigns for ever AND I give and devise
unto my Nephew Thomas Brocklehurst of Hurdsfield aforesaid Silk
Manufacturer and Banker ALL my messuages cottages and tenements with
the lands hereditaments and appurtenances thereunto respectively
belonging situate and lying and being in Cheadle Buckley and Cheadle
Moseley in the said County now in the several occupations of Widow
Fawkner James Fisher and Daniel Adamson as tenants thereof AND also
all that my messuage and tenement with the lands hereditaments and
appurtenances thereunto belonging situate lying and being in the
Township of Marple in the said County now in the occupations of John
Beaumont and --- Cooper as tenants thereof AND also all that my
messuage and tenement with the lands hereditaments and appurtenances
thereunto belonging situate near Hazle Grove and in the Borough of
Stockport aforesaid now in the occupation of Thomas Hallworth as

tenant thereof AND also two yearly chief rents of seven pounds eight shillings and four pounds issuing and payable from Land in the said Borough of Stockport which I lately leased to Isaac Smith and Thomas Smith AND also all the yearly chief rents in the Borough of Stockport aforesaid which I purchased from Lord Vernon's Trustees AND also another yearly chief rent of Eleven pounds five shillings issuing and payable from a plot of land in Cheadle Buckley aforesaid lately leased by me to Lord Vernon and used as a Coal Wharf TO HOLD the same to the said Thomas Brocklehurst his heirs and assigns for ever AND all the rest residue and remainder of my real estate and chief rents whatsoever and whensoever not hereinbefore by me disposed of AND all my personal estate and effects whatsoever and wheresoever that I shall die possessed of or entitled to after payment of all my just debts and funeral and testamentary expences as aforesaid I give devise and bequeath to my said Nephews William Brocklehurst John Brocklehurst and Thomas Brocklehurst their heirs executors administrators and assigns for ever equally share and share alike as tenants in common and not as joint tenants AND I APPOINT the said William Brocklehurst John Brocklehurst and Thomas Brocklehurst Executors of this my Will AND hereby revoking all former and other Will and Wills by me at any time heretofore made I make and declare this to be my last Will and Testament IN WITNESS whereof the said Peter Pownall the Testator have hereunto set my hand the day and year first before written -- Peter Pownall -- Signed by the said Testator Peter Pownall as and for his last Will and Testament in the presence of us at the same time who at his request and in his presence and in the presence of each other have hereunto subscribed our names as Witnesses -- P P Brocklehurst Macclesfield -- Thomas Rhodes Bramhall.

I PETER POWNALL of Bramhall in the County of Chester Esquire do make this as a Codicil to my last Will and Testament and direct that the same shall be taken as part thereof I give and bequeath the following legacies that is to say To my Housekeeper - Dawson £100 To Isaac Booth farm Laboror £80 To The Reverend Mr Colston £5 To - Rhodes Farm Laboror £20 to Mrs - Lomas £10 To Moses Lomas £6 To Rachel (my House Servant) £6 To Charles Bennett £6 To John Moult £6 and which legacies I hereby direct shall be paid by my Executors free of legacy duty IN WITNESS whereof I the said Peter Pownall have hereunto set and subscribed my name this 20th day of October one thousand eight hundred and fifty eight - Peter Pownall Signed by the said Peter Pownall as and for a Codicil to his last Will and Testament in the presence of us present at the same time who at his request in his presence and in the presence of each other have hereunto subscribed our names as for: 13 Chancery
witnesses P P Brocklehurst - G P Mellor

       I Hereby Certify that the foregoing is a true copy of the original Will and Codicil the same having been carefully compared therewith

Appendix 5d

THE POWNALL FAMILY GRAVESTONES at St Marys Parish Church, Stockport

There are two gravestones

TO THE MEMORY OF PETER POWNALL of Bramhall who departed this life August 12 1791 aged 84 years   [? He is the father of the author of the diary,   and is reported in William Pownall's will as under 21 in 1736].   Also JANE,   wife of PETER POWNALL,   who departed this life July 17th 1752 aged 26 years.   Also ALICE wife of PETER POWNALL, who departed this life April 10th 1785 aged 82 years [? Mentioned in the diary 1 June 1786. It is thought that these details refer to a Betty Pownall   of Poynton,   wife to a   different   Peter Pownall].   Also WILLIAM,   their   son who departed this life July 20th 1806   aged   35 years.   Also BENJAMIN POWNALL,   brother of the above PETER POWNALL, who   departed this life November 4th 1785 aged 63   years.   [Actually died 1 November]

This Grave belongs to the representatives of the late PETER   POWNALL Esq of Pownall Green, Bramhall

TO THE MEMORY OF ALICE POWNALL of Bramhall who departed this   life December   1st   1831 aged 63 years.   MARY POWNALL   of   Bramhall   who departed this life February 28th 1833 Aged 59 years.   PETER POWNALL son   of   PETER   POWNALL and brother to the above   of   Pownall   Green Bramhall who departed this life November 3rd 1858 in the 94 year   of his age.

This Vault belongs to the legal Representatives of the late PETER POWNALL Esq of Pownall Green Bramhall

APPENDIX 5e

THE WILL AND INVENTORY OF WILLIAM POWNALL   (Grandfather   of   the author of the diary)

THE WILL (Dated 18 March 1736)

In the Name God Amen I WILLIAM POWNALL of Bromhall in the County of Chester Yeoman being something Indisposed as to my bodily health but of Sound and Disposeing mind and understanding praised be God for it For   the   preventing of suits and Differences amongst   my   wife   and Children after my Decease Doe make and Declare this my last Will and Testament in manner and form following -
First I recommend my Soul into the hands of God my Saviour in hopes of a Joyfull resurrection, my body, I also recommend to a Decent yet plain   interment   according   to the Discretion of my   Wife,   and   my Executors   herein afternamed.   As touching such worldly Estates   it hath   pleased God of his Goodness to bless me with,   I   dispose   the same   as   follows First I charge all that my Messuage,   Lands   and hereditament Scituate lyeing and being in Bromhall aforesaid,   with

the payment of all such Debts as are now already lodged therein by Mortgage as also with the sume of Three Hundred pounds sterling to be paid for such at such times and in such manner as is herein after mentioned. Also I give and devise to my son JOHN POWNALL the said Messuage Lands and hereditaments (his heirs) and to his assignes upon condition that he shall and Do pay all Such debts and the said sume of three hundred pounds I have charged thereupon as above said And as concerning the Disposicion of the sume of Three hundred Pounds charged on my said Messuage and Land as aforesaid. I dispose of the same as follows, that is to say I give and bequeath to my son PETER POWNALL One Hundred Pounds part thereof Also I give and bequeath to my Daughter MARY POWNALL One Hundred pounds part thereof Also I give and bequeath to my Daughter ELIZABETH POWNALL One Hundred Pounds residue thereof And I doe hereby Will and Order that the said legacies be paid to my said son and Daughters as they shall severally attain to the full Age of One and Twenty years. Also in case either of my said Daughters shall die before thay attain One and Twenty Years of Age - Then I give and bequeath the legacy or share of her soe dying unto my said son JOHN POWNALL And also I charge that my messuage Lands and hereditaments scituate and lying and being within the Liberty of High Legh in the said County of Chester that I hold in the right of Mary my wife with the sume of One Hundred Pounds sterling to be paid within the space of Twelve Kalendar months next Ensueing together after the Decease of my said wife to and for such as is herein aftermentioned. That is to say I give and bequeath to my son BENJAMIN POWNALL the said sume of One Hundred pounds if he shall have attained to the full [age interlined] of one and twenty years (of age) at my wife's Decease. And as concerning my Personal Estate I Dispose of the Same as follows. That is to say It is my mind and Will that all my Debts (Except such as are Lodged and charged to be paid out of my real Estate as herein before mencioned) my funeral Expences and probate of this my Last will be paid and first discharged out of my said personal Estate Also the rest and remainder of my said personal Estate I give and bequeath to my said son JOHN POWNALL Also it is further my mind and Will that if my said sons or daughters shall be discontented with the provision by me hereby made for them and shall raise or Commence any Suits or Actions Against my Executors or One Against Another In such case each of them shall prove so litigious or troublesome shall there by forfeit and lose all his, her and their share of my said estate hereby given, devised and bequeathed to him her or them respectively and in lieu thereof shall have only a several sume of One Guinea out of it, and no more and the residue to be equally divided amongst the rest of my children Also - this my last Will and Testament I appoint my Brother PETER POWNALL and my son JOHN POWNALL executors hopeing they will faithfully perform the trust I have reposed in them. And I do hereby revoke all former Wills And in Testimony that this is my last Will and Testament I have hereunto put my hand and seal the eighteenth day of March in the year of our Lord One thousand Seven Hundred and Thirty Six.

William Pownall [signed]

Sealed Signed and Published and Declared by the said William Pownall the Testator to be his last Will and Testament in the presence of us Hellen Smith Sarah Booth ?Thos Jannion [all signed]

APPENDIX 5e (cont)

THE INVENTORY OF WILLIAM POWNALL (dated 2 April 1737)

A true Inventory of all the Goods Cattle and Chattells of William
Pownall late of Bromhall in the County of Chester Yeoman Deceased
Appraised and Valued by Thomas Taylor and Peter Ridgway both of
Bromhall aforesaid Yeoman on the second Day of April in the Year of
our Lord 1737

	£	s	d
First in Cattle	63	10	0
In Husbandry Ware	16	16	6
In Corn and Hay	53	2	0
Boards	1	5	0
Two Swine	1	10	0
In Cheese	50	0	0
In the highest Chamber			
One pair of Bedstocks and Beding	3	0	0
Another pair of Bedstocks and Beding	3	0	0
In the Best Chamber			
One pair of Bedstocks and Beding	5	10	0
Two Chairs	0	2	6
In Linnens	7	8	0
Another pair of Bedstocks and Beding	3	10	0
One Back Stoole and a Coffer	0	7	0
In Bacon	2	10	0
In the Kitchen			
A Salting Turnel	1	0	0
In Coopers Ware	1	9	0
One Cheese Press	1	0	0
One Crab-press		10	0
One Kneading Turnell	0	3	0
One Brass boyler	1	0	0
One Iron boyler	0	12	0
One iron Pott	0	4	0
One Table and a forme	0	4	0
In the Buttery			
In Earthen Ware	0	4	6
In Cheese Facts	0	10	0
One Dozen of Trenchers	0	1	6
A Chaffing Dish	0	2	6
In Pewter	0	8	0
A Driping Pan	0	2	6
In the Parlour			
One pair of Bedstocks and Beding	6	10	0
One Chest of Drawers	2	0	0
8 Back Stools and Looking Glass	1	4	0
4 Spining wheels	0	8	0

<u>In the house</u>

A Dresser Shelves and Pewter	5	10	0
One Clock and Case	2	10	0
3 Couch Chairs and 2 Back Stools	1	3	6
7 Rush bottomed chairs	0	6	0
A warming Pan, Spit and Goberts	0	11	0
A frying Pan and some small Iron things	0	6	0
Pot-wracks and the Sweey	0	2	6
One Brass Pott knives and Forks	0	8	0
Weighs weights sacks and Bags	1	18	0
In Old Iron	0	10	0
In potatoes		6	0
Owing to the Deceadant	150	0	0
The Deceadants Purse and Apparrel	7	0	0
In Hustlements	0	10	0
Omitted above in the Parlour an Oval Table	1	0	0
	403	0	0

Apprized by Thomas Taylor and Peter Ridgway   [signed]

The inventory lists the rooms in the hall.   The main living room is called the "house" where most of the cooking was probably done. The parlour was also a bedroom, and housed the spinning wheels and an "Oval Table" (see Appendix 5f, Peter Pownall the Elder's Inventory). The kitchen appears to have been used for food preservation, and possibly brewing, etc. ("Coopers Ware" would have been **staved** utensils;   the buttery seems to have been used as a dairy where butter and a considerable amount of **cheese** were made.   The chambers were usually upstairs rooms, one of which, although considered "The Best Chamber" and probably William's bedroom, was also used to store the bacon. "Hustlements" were all those useful little items too small to specify.

Ref WS 1737 Cheshire County Record Office

APPENDIX 5f

THE WILL AND THE INVENTORY OF PETER POWNALL THE ELDER (Brother of the above William)

THE WILL (Dated 5 May 1750)

IN THE NAME OF GOD AMEN I Peter Pownall the Elder of Bromhall in the County of Chester Gentleman being something indisposed as to my bodily Health but of sound and perfect mind memory and understanding praised be God for the same. Do make and publish this my last will and Testament in manner and form following, That is to Say, First I will and order that all my Debts (if any be) funeral Expences and the probate of this my last Will and Testament be first paid and discharged out of my whole personal Estate. Also I give and devise unto my Nephew Peter Pownall all that my Messuage Tenement Lands and Hereditaments called or known by the Name or Names of Holts other- wise Brown's Tenement with part of Birkenstale's Tenement joyned with it in purchase in the Original purchase Deed, all situate lying and being in Bromhall afores[ai]d (Except a small parcel of Ground lately inclosed of the Common) To Hold the said premises and every part and parcel thereof except as before Excepted, unto my said Nephew Peter Pownall and his Assignes during his natural Life, and from and after his Decease to his Male Issue of his body lawfully begotten, preferring the Elder before the younger, and in default of such Issue to my Nephew Benjamin Pownall his Heirs and Assignes for ever Under and upon Condition that my said Nephew Peter Pownall pay unto my Nephew John Pownall or his Assignes the sum of two Hundred pounds within the Space of one whole year next after my Decease, which said Sum of two Hundred Pounds I give unto my said Nephew John Pownall. ALSO the residue and remainder of my [mes]suages and Lands Scituate lying and being in Bromhall afores[ai]d I give and devise unto my said Nephew John Pownall. To hold the said premises and every part and parcel thereof unto my said Nephew John Pownall and his assignes during his natural Life, and from and after his Decease to the Male Issue of his body lawfully begotten, preferring the Elder before the younger and in default of such Issue - to my said Nephew Peter Pownall and his Assignes during his natural Life And from and after his Decease to the Male Issue of his Body Lawfully begotten, preferring the Elder before the younger and in default of such Issue - - to my said Nephew Benjamin Pownall his Heirs and Assignes for ever, Subject nevertheless to the uses heretofore men- tioned Also I give and bequeath unto my Brother Samuel Pownall one shilling. Also I give and bequeath unto my Nieces Mary Murray and Elizabeth Mottram if both or one of them become widows - - each Five Pounds a year during their joint or respective Widowhood but no longer Also I give and bequeath unto my Nephew or Cousin John Mottram Eighty Pounds towards binding him out Apprentice and setting him up, twenty pounds part thereof to be paid when he is bound if so much be then required and sixty pounds residue of the s[ai]d Eighty Pounds at the Expiration of his Apprenticeship. Also I will and Order that the pecuniary Legacy already bequeathed shall be paid by my said Nephew John Pownall his Heirs or Assigns out of that part of my Real Estate herein before given and Devised to him as afore-

113

s[ai]d. And all the residue and remainder of my personal Estate of
what kind or Quality soever. I give and bequeath unto my said
Nephew John Pownall on Condition he pays all my Debts but particularly to clear of a Bond Debt of Six Hundred and Sixty pounds
formerly given by me unto my Brother Benjamin Pownal and the sum of
ten pounds to be distributed amongst the poor by my Executor hereafter Named but not a busy Funeral but at such Time and times and in
such Manner as they discretionally shall think proper. And lastly I
do hereby Nominate and appoint my s[ai]d Nephews John Pownal and
Peter Pownall Executors of this my last Will and Testament hereby
revoking all former Wills by me heretofore made and declare this to
be my last Will and Testament. In Witness thereof I have herein put
my Hand and Seal this fifth day of May in the Year of Our Lord one
thousand seven Hundred and fifty.

Peter Pownall [signed and sealed]

Sealed signed and published .. in the presence of us
    John Booth Ann Booth T Jannion
                11th October 1751

John Pownall and Peter Pownall the Ex[ecu]tors above named were
sworn in comon form before   Abel Ward [signed]

INVENTORY OF PETER POWNALL THE ELDER

Peter Pownall the Elder appears to have been living in part of a
house as only two rooms are specified. Whether this was Pownall
Hall we cannot say, although it was common for ageing relatives to
live with their families. Several of the items in the Parlour seem
to be the same as those in the inventory above (Appendix 5e).
Compared with other inventories of the same period in Bramhall he
has some valuable items including a wider selection of furniture,
silver and books etc than usual.

A true Inventory of the Goods of Master Peter Pownall of Bramhall in
the County of Chester Deceased   [no date Died 1751]

	£	s	d
In the Chamber			
A Bed and what belongs to it	2	10	0
A Escritoire	2	0	0
A Chest of Drawers	1	15	0
A Look Glass	0	2	6
A Seeling Table		4	0
A Corner Cupboard	0	5	0
A parcel of Books	2	0	0
A Dozen of Chairs	1	4	0
A Chest	0	12	0

In the Parlour

A Corner Cupboard & Salt pye	0	6	0
A silver Tankard & Spoon	4	10	0
Seven Backstools	1	8	0
A Looking Glass	0	6	8
A Oval Table	0	5	0
Three pictures	0	5	0
A little Round Table	0	2	0
four pair of Sheets	2	10	0
Purse and Apparel	12	0	0
A Silver Watch	1	10	0
a fire Iron & Guard	0	5	0
Some odd Timber	0	2	6
	34	2	8

Valued and appraised
by Us   George Hulme
         Tho[mas] Taylor

Ref WS 1751 Cheshire County Record Office

Appendix 5g

ABSTRACT FROM **THE WILL OF JOHN POWNALL** (Son of the above William).

Dated 17 March 1775

In the name of God Amen I **John Pownall** of Bromhall in the County of
Chester Yeoman being somewhat under Affliction of Body Yet (through
the Mercy of God) of good and perfect Sound Disposing mind and Memory and Understanding But calling to mind the Uncertainty of my Time
in this World and in order to settle my Temporal affairs do make and
Ordain this my last Will and Testament in manner following (That   is
to Say) and first it is my Will and Mind and I do hereby Direct and
appoint that all my Just Debts Funeral Expenses and the Charge of
proving this my Will shall be paid and Discharged out of my personal
Estate and as for and Concerning all my Estate and Effects of what
Nature or kind soever wherewith it hath pleased God to bestow upon
me I Dispose of the same as follows and First I charge my Real and
Personal Estates with the payment of such Legacies and bequests as I
shall hereafter particularly Mention (That is to say) That the Sum
of One Hundred and ninety Pounds Arising therefrom shall be placed
out at Interest Immediately after my Death and I Do hereby Charge my
said Estates with the Raising the same by such Means as my Executors
hereafter Named shall think meet and the Interest Arising therefore
not Exceeding four pounds for One Hundred pounds and proportionably
thereunto I will and Direct that my said Executors Do pay and apply
to the Use and behoof of my **Brother Benjamin Pownal** as the same
shall become Due and payable Yearly During his Natural Life or in
such other sort and manner as they or the Survivor of them shall

115

think meet and from And after the Death of my said **Brother Benjamin
Pownal** then I give and bequeath unto my Nephews **William Pownall John
Pownall and Peter Pownall** Sons of my said **Brother Benjamin Pownal**
each the Sum of Fifty pounds and to my Nieces **Mary Pownall** and **Eliz-
abeth Pownall** Daughters of my said **Brother Benjamin Pownal** each the
sum of Twenty pounds Also I Give and Bequeath unto My Nephews and
Nieces **John Murrey Nathaniel Murray Josiah Murrey** and **Mary Murrey**
each the sum of Twenty pounds Also I give and bequeath unto my
Nephews and Nieces **John Mottram Pownall Mottram Mary Mottram Ann
Mottram** and **Sarah Mottram** Sons and Daughters of my Brother in law
Peter Mottram by my **Sister Elizabeth** his Late Wife Deseased each the
sum of Twenty pounds all which said Legacies I will shall be paid to
my said Nephews and Nieces ..... after the Death of my said Brother
Benjamin Pownal or to such of them as shall then have attained the
Age of Twenty One Years ..... Etc ..... after the Death of my said
Brother **Benjamin Pownal** then I give and bequeath unto my Nephews
William Pownall John Pownall and **Peter Pownall** sons of my said
Brother **Benjamin Pownal** each the Sum of Fifty Pounds and to my
Nieces **Mary Pownall** and **Elizabeth Pownall** Daughters of my said
Brother **Benjamin Pownal** each the sum of Twenty Pounds Also I give
and Bequeath unto my Nephews and Nieces **John Murrey Nathaniel Murrey
Josiah Murrey** and **Mary Murrey** each the sum of Twenty Pounds Also I
Give and bequeath to my Nephews and Nieces **John Mottram Pownall
Mottram Mary Mottram** and **Sarah Mottram** Sons and Daughters of my
Brother in law **Peter Mottram** by my **Sister Elizabeth** his Late Wife
Deceased each the sum of Twenty Pounds .. Also Give and Bequeath
unto my Brother in law **Nathaniel Murrey** whom I shall herein appoint
One of my Executors to this my will The Sum of Twenty pounds for and
as a Gratuity for the Trouble he may be put unto in and by reason of
the Trust by me in him Reposed ..... All the Residue and Remainder
of my Estates Both Real and personal ..... unto my Brother **Peter
Pownall** ..... I Nominate Constitute and Appoint my said **Brother
Peter Pownall** and my **Brother-in-law Nathaniel Murrey** Executors .....
In Witness whereof I have ..... put my hand and Seal the Seventeenth
Day of March in the Year of Our Lord One Thousand Seven Hundred and
Sixty Nine .....
             John Pownall   [signed and sealed]

[Witnessed by]
Samuel Bennett   Ann Peett   William Storrs

This will was particularly useful for the evidence of the members of
the family. Because of its length only the relevant parts have been
printed. A full transcript of the original is deposited at Stockport Library

Ref WS 1775 Cheshire County Record Office.

APPENDIX 6

SOME FAMILY TREES

We have not carried out extensive research into the family trees so they should be regarded only as an indication of the families. We are indebted to Mrs P Litton, family historian, for her advice.

EVIDENCE OF POWNALLS IN BRAMHALL

We have traced references to the following Pownalls in Bramhall but are unable to prove they were ancestors of Peter Pownall.

1443   Edmund Pownall, juror, signed an Inquisition Post Mortem.

1445   Edmund and Robert Pownall listed as "Knights, Gentlemen and Freeholders". Also in lease from Geoffrey de Mottershead.

1518   Robert Pownall (See POWNALL FAMILY)

1586   Burial of Anne, daughter of Richard Pownall

1587   Burial of Ales, wife of Richard Pownall

1591/2 Burial of Richard Pownall

1604   Death of Humphrey Pownall. He had a natural son John Hey, who in turn had a natural son Francis, alias Hey, alias Shrigley, by Faith Shrigley (living c 1664). Francis subsequently had a son, William.

1623/4 John (Heys) Pownall leased lands from William Davenport, previously held by his father, Humphrey Pownall.

1632   John Pownall was **moorlooker** for Kitts Moor.

1642   John, Humphrey and Francis Pownall. (See POWNALL FAMILY)

1645   John, Humphrey and Francis Pownall were jurors at **Bramhall Court**.

1664   Francis Pownall leased lands from William Davenport lately held by his father John. The lease includes William Pownall, son of Francis. It is possible that this William may be Peter Pownall's grandfather. See Appendix 5e

APPENDIX 6a

THE POWNALL FAMILY TREE

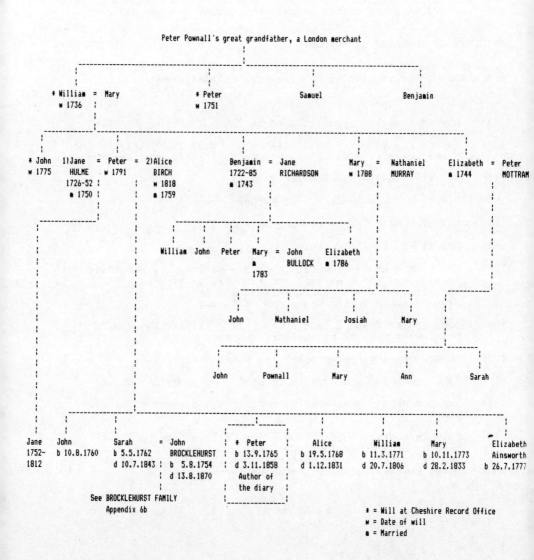

Peter Pownall's great grandfather, a London merchant

* William = Mary   * Peter   Samuel   Benjamin
w 1736   w 1751

* John   1)Jane = Peter = 2)Alice   Benjamin = Jane   Mary   = Nathaniel   Elizabeth = Peter
w 1775   HULME   w 1791   BIRCH   1722-85   RICHARDSON w 1788   MURRAY   a 1744   MOTTRAM
         1726-52   w 1818   a 1743
         a 1750   a 1759

                            William John Peter Mary = John   Elizabeth
                                                  a   BULLOCK   a 1786
                                                  1783

                                      John   Nathaniel   Josiah   Mary

                              John   Pownall   Mary   Ann   Sarah

Jane   John   Sarah   = John   * Peter   Alice   William   Mary   Elizabeth
1752-   b 10.8.1760   b 5.5.1762   BROCKLEHURST   b 13.9.1765   b 19.5.1768 b 11.3.1771 b 10.11.1773 Ainsworth
1812   d 10.7.1843   b 5.8.1754   d 3.11.1858   d 1.12.1831 d 20.7.1806 d 28.2.1833 b 26.7.1777
                                    d 13.8.1870   Author of
                                                   the diary

                      See BROCKLEHURST FAMILY
                         Appendix 6b

                                                               * = Will at Cheshire Record Office
                                                               w = Date of will
                                                               a = Married

118

APPENDIX 6b

THE BROCKLEHURST FAMILY TREE

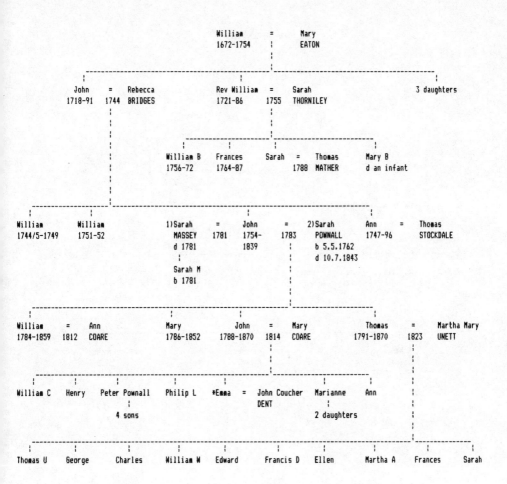

* Emma Dent was the author of <u>IN MEMORY OF JOHN BROCKLEHURST</u> 1897.
Further details of the family tree can be found in <u>EAST CHESHIRE</u>
Earwaker vol ii pp 423/4

APPENDIX 6c

THE HARDY FAMILY TREE

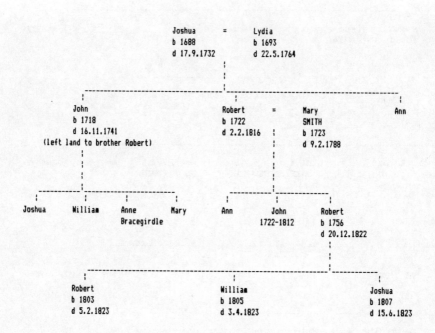

THE HARDY FAMILY TREE

```
                              Joshua      =      Lydia
                              b 1688             b 1693
                              d 17.9.1732        d 22.5.1764

         --------------------------------------------------------------------
         |                            |                              |
        John                        Robert    =    Mary             Ann
        b 1718                      b 1722         SMITH
        d 16.11.1741               d 2.2.1816      b 1723
   (left land to brother Robert)                   d 9.2.1788

    -----------------------------------        -------------------------------
    |        |         |          |            |          |              |
 Joshua   William    Anne       Mary          Ann       John          Robert
                   Bracegirdle                        1722-1812       b 1756
                                                                     d 20.12.1822

                 ------------------------------------------------------
                 |                          |                         |
              Robert                     William                   Joshua
              b 1803                     b 1805                    b 1807
              d 5.2.1823                 d 3.4.1823                d 15.6.1823
```

120

BIBLIOGRAPHY

LOCAL & FAMILY HISTORY

AIKIN, J A Description of the Country from Thirty to Forty Miles
    round Manchester (1793, Reprinted 1968)
ANDREWS, C B (Ed) The Torrington Diaries 1781-1794 (1934-1938)
    Vols 2 & 3
ANGUS-BUTTERWORTH, L M   Old Cheshire Families and Their Seats (1932
    Reprinted 1970)
ASHMORE, Owen The Industrial Archaeology of Stockport (1975)
ASPIN, C Lancashire the First Industrial Society (1969)
ASTLE, William (Ed) The History of Stockport (1922, 1932 & 1971)
ASTON, Joseph A Picture of Manchester (1969)
BAGLEY, J J History of Lancashire (1956 Reprinted 1970)
BAGSHAW, S History, Gazetteer and Directory of the County Palatine
    of Chester (1850)
BECK, Joan Tudor Cheshire (1969)
BODY, A H Canals and Waterways (1975)
BURGESS, Rev. W H The Story of Dean Row Chapel (1924)
CLEMENSHA, H W The New Court Book of the Manor at Bramhall 1632-
    -1657 Ch Soc New Series Vol 80 (1921)
CORRIE, Andrew An Illustrated History of Methodism in Bramhall
    (1971)
COUNTY COURT ROLLS Ch Soc Vol 84
COUTIE, Heather (Ed) Hazel Grove or Bullock Smithy (1982)
COUTIE, Heather (Ed) Hazel Grove T'Other End O' Village (1985)
COWHIG, W T Textiles (1976)
CROZIER, Mary An Old Silk Family 1745-1945: The Brocklehursts of
    Brocklehurst, Whiston, Amalgamated, Ltd. (1947)
DAVIES, C Stella (Ed) A History of Macclesfield (1961 Reprinted
    1981)
DEAN, E Barbara Bramall Hall: the Story of an Elizabethan Manor
    House (1977)
DEAN, E Barbara Bygone Bramhall (1980)
DEAN, E Barbara The Owners of Bramall Hall Cheshire History No 2
    (1978)
DEAN ROW UNITARIAN CHAPEL Wilmslow Historical Society (1976)
DENT, Emma In Memory of John Brocklehurst (1897)
DODGSON, J McN The Place-Names of Cheshire Vol 1 (1970)
DORE, R N The Civil Wars in Cheshire (1966)
DRIVER, J T Cheshire in the Later Middle Ages (1971)
EARWAKER, J P East Cheshire: 2 Vols (1880-90)
GAUTREY, Arthur J The Early Days of Knutsford Gaol Cheshire History
    No 1 (1978)
GRINDON, Leo H Manchester Banks and Bankers (1877)
HARLAND, H & WILKINSON, T T Lancashire Folk Lore
HARRIS, Brian E (Ed) The Victoria History of Cheshire Vol 1 (1987)
    Vol 2 (1979) & Vol 3 (1979)
HEGINBOTHAM, H Stockport Ancient and Modern 2 Vols (1882 & 1892)
HEWITT, H J Cheshire Under the Three Edwards (1967)

BIBLIOGRAPHY

HODSON, Howard   Cheshire 1660-1780: Restoration to Industrial Revol-
     ution (1978)
HODSON, Howard   The Story of Wilmslow (1971)
HUSAIN, B M C   Cheshire Under the Norman Earls (1973)
INGHAM, Alfred   Cheshire: Its Tradition and History (1877 Reprinted
     1973)
MITCHELL, Frank and Teretta   Gatley: A Pictorial History of the
     Parish of St James the Apostle (1980)
MITCHELL, S I   Food Shortages and Public Order in Cheshire 1757-1812
     T L C A S Vol 81 1982
MORRILL, J S   Cheshire 1630-1660: County Government during the
     English Revolution (1974)
MORRILL, J S & Dore, R N   The Allegiance of Cheshire Gentry in the
     Great Civil War   T L C A S   75-76 (1965-1966)
MORRIS John (Gen Ed)   The Domesday Book, Cheshire   Ed Morgan, Philip
     (1978)
MOSS, Fletcher   A History of the Old Parish of Cheadle in Cheshire
     (2n Ed 1970)
NICHOLSON, J Holme   The Ancient Presbyterian Chapel at Dean Row
     Cheshire T L C A S   Vol 10 (1892)
NICKSON, Charles   Bygone Altrincham: Traditions and History (1935)
ORMEROD, George   The History of the County Palatine and City of
     Chester. 3 Vols (1819, 2nd Ed 1882, Republished 1980, Vol 3 The
     Hundred of Macclesfield)
PEARSON, Andrew   Wilmslow Past and Present (1901 Reprinted 1972)
PEVSNER, Nikolaus   Cheshire   Buildings of England (1971)
PHILLIPS C B & SMITH, J H (Eds)   Stockport Probate Records 1578-1619
     R S L C   Vol CXXIV (1985)
QUARTER SESSIONS RECORDS 1559-1760   T R S L C Vol 94 (1940)
RAFFALD, Elizabeth   Directory of Manchester and Salford (1772
     Reprinted 1889 & ? 1980s)
RIPLEY, D   The Peak Forest Tramway   (1972)
SHERCLIFF, W H   Poynton Park: Its Lords and their Mansions (1988)
SHERCLIFF, W H   Manchester, a Short History of Its Development (4th
     Ed 1972)
SHERCLIFF, W H, KITCHING, D A & RYAN, J M   Poynton, a Coalmining
     Village; Social History, Transport and Industry 1700-1939
     (1983)
SILVERWOOD, Derek   Pownall Green School, Bramhall 1877-1977 (1977)
SMITH, H D & GORDON, E J   A Short History of the Parish and Church
     of St Michael & All Angels Bramhall 1910-1970 (1970)
SQUIRE, Carole   Cheadle Hulme: a Brief History (1976)
SYLVESTER, Dorothy   A History of Cheshire (1971, 2nd Ed 1980)
SYLVESTER, Dorothy & Nulty, Geoffrey (Eds)   The Historical Atlas of
     Cheshire (1958 Revised 1966)
TAYLOR, W M P   A History of the Stockport Court Leet (1971)
UNWIN, George   Samuel Oldknow and the Arkwrights (1924 2nd Ed 1967)
WAINWRIGHT, Joel   Memories of Marple (1899)

ENGLISH SOCIAL HISTORY

ASPIN, Chris The Cotton Industry (1981)
BEALE, C H (Ed) Reminiscences of a Gentlewoman of the Last Century:
    the Letters of Catherine Hutton
BENSON, Anna P Textile Machines (1983)
BLACK'S Dictionary of Medicine (1906 New Edition 1987)
BREWER'S Dictionary of Phrase and Fable (1870 Revised 1952)
BURGHALL, Edward Diary (c1628)
CARTER, Harold B Sir Joseph Banks (1988)
CLARK, Peter The English Alehouse: A Social History, 1200-1830
    (1983)
COBBETT, William Cottage Economy (1821 Reprinted 1978)
CUNNINGHAM, P & LUCAS, C Costume for Births, Marriages and Deaths
FEARN, Jaqueline Domestic Bygones (1977)
FIENNES, Celia The Journeys of Celia Fiennes (Ed C Morris (1947)
HARRISON, Molly People and Furniture (1971)
HARTLEY, Dorothy Land of England (1979)
HOLE, C Ed British Folk Customs (New Ed 1978)
HORN, Pamela The Rural World 1780-1851 (1983)
IREDALE, David Discovering Local History (1973 & 1977)
JEWELL, Brian Fairs and Revels (1976)
LAVER, James A Concise History of Costume (1969)
LEADBEATER, Eliza Spinning and Spinning Wheels (1979)
LOVETT, Maurice Brewing and Breweries (1981)
MACFARLANE A Guide to English Historical Sources (1983)
MARWICK, Arthur (Gen Ed) The Illustrated Dictionary of British
    History (1980)
MINGAY, Gordon E English Landed Society in the 18th Century (1963)
MITCHELL, B R Abstract of British Historical Statistics (1962)
MORSLEY, Clifford News from the English Countryside 1750-1850
    (1979)
PARKER, R The Common Stream (1976)
ROSE, M E English Poor Law 1730-1930 (1971)
SALAMAN, R N The History and Social Influence of the Potato (1970)
SASS, Lorna To the Queen's Taste (1977)
SEYMOUR, John The Forgotten Arts (1984)
SHIRLEY, E English Deer Parks (1867)
SMITH, D J Discovering Country Crafts (1977)
WALKER, Kenneth The Story of Medicine
WILDEBLOOD, Jan The Polite World
WOODFORDE, James The Diary of a Country Parson 1758-1802 (Reprinted
    1948)
YARWOOD, Doreen The English Home

LOCAL HISTORY RESEARCH

CHENEY, C R (Ed) Handbook of Dates for Students of English History
    (1978)
FISHER, John L A Medieval Farming Glossary of Latin and English
    Words. (1968)

BIBLIOGRAPHY

GRIEVE, E P Examples of English Handwriting 1150-1750 (1954
    Reprinted 1981)
HOSKINS, W G Fieldwork in Local History (1967 2nd Ed 1982))
HOSKINS, W G Local History in England (1972)
LEIGH, Egerton A A Glossary of Words used in the Dialect of
    Cheshire (1877)
MILLWARD, Rosemary A Glossary of Household, Farming and Trade Terms
    from Probate Inventories (1987 Revised 1982)
RICHARDSON, John The Local Historian's Encyclopedia (1974 Reprinted
    1986)
ROGERS, Alan Approaches to Local History (1972)
ROGERS, Alan (Ed) Group Projects in Local History (1977)
STEPHENS, William B Sources for English Local History (2nd Ed 1981)
TATE, W The Parish Chest (1969 Reprinted 1983)
WALSH, Audrey C & Allan, Adrian R The History of the County Palat-
    ine of Chester: A Short Bibliography and Guide to Sources
    (1983)
WRIGHT, Peter The Cheshire Chatter (1974)

AGRICULTURE

ADDY, John The Agrarian Revolution (1964)
BLACK'S Veterinary Dictionary
BRADLEY, R The Country Gentleman and Farmer's Monthly Director
    (1726)
BRIGDEN, Roy Agricultural Hand Tools (1983)
BUTCHER, Thomas K Country Life (1970)
CASH, R C The Benefit of Marl, Cheshire's Natural Inheritance
    Cheshire History Newsletter No 10 (1976)
CHALONER, W H (Ed) The Reminiscences of Richard Lindop, Farmer
    (1778-1871) T L C A S Vol LV (1940)
CHAMBERS, J D & MINGAY, G E The Agricultural Revolution 1750-1880
    (1966)
CHARLTON, Kenneth James Cropper (1773-1840) and Agricultural
    Improvement in the Early 19C T H S L C Vol 112 (1961)
COBBETT, William Rural Rides (1830)
COLLINS The Pocket Guide to Wild Flowers (1955)
DANSON, J T Agriculture in Cheshire (1854)
DAVIES, C Stella The Agricultural History of Cheshire 1750-1850
    Ch Soc 3rd Series Vol 10 (1960)
ERNLE, Lord English Farming Past and Present (1961 6th Edition)
FELL, W Agriculture of Cheshire (1833)
FIELD, J English Field Names: A Dictionary (1972)
FUSSELL, G E Four Centuries of Cheshire Farming Systems 1500-1900
    T H S L C Vol 106 (1955)
FUSSELL, G E The Story of Farming (1969)
GILES, Phyllis Enclosure of Common Lands in Stockport T L C A S
    LX11 (1950-51)
GRANT, I F Highland Folk Ways (1961 Reprinted 1980)
HALL, David Medieval Fields (1982)
HARVEY, Nigel Fields, Hedges and Ditches (1976)

HOLLAND, Henry A General View of the Agriculture of Cheshire
    (1808)
HOSKINS, W G English Landscapes (1973)
INGRAM, Arthur Dairying Bygones (1987)
JONES, E L Agriculture and Economic Growth in England 1650-1815
    (1967)
KERRIDGE, E The Agricultural Revolution (1967)
MAJOR, J Kenneth Animal-Powered Machines (1985)
MATHIAS, P The Transformation of England (1979)
MERCER, W B Two Centuries of Cheshire Cheese Farming J R A S
    Vol 98 (1937)
MINGAY, George E Enclosure and the Small Farmer (1968)
MORTIMER, J The Whole Art of Husbandry Vol 1 (1716)
PALIN, William Cheshire; a Report on the Agriculture J R A S
    Vol 5 (1848)
POLLARD, E, Hooper, M D, Moore, NW Hedges (1974)
PORTER, R E The Marketing of Agricultural Produce in Cheshire
    During the 19th Century T H S L C Vol 126 (1976)
PORTER, R E The Value of Farm Noterbooks: A New Example from
    Cheshire. The Local Historian Vol 13 (1979)
SCARD, Geoffrey Squire and Tenant: Rural Life in Cheshire 1760-1900
    (1981)
SMITH, D J Discovering Horse-drawn Farm Macinery (1979)
SYLVESTER, Dorothy The Open Fields of Cheshire T H S L C CVIII
    (1956)
TAYLOR, C Fields in the English Landscape (1975)
TROW SMITH, R A History of British Livestock Husbandry 1700-1900
    (1959)
TYLDEN, G Discovering Harness and Saddlery (1971)
WEDGE, T A A General View of the Agriculture of the County Palatine
    of Chester Board of Agriculture (1794)
WHITE, Gilbert The Natural History of Selborne (1788-9 Reprinted
    1962)
WHITING, J R S History at Source: Agriculture 1730-1872
YOUNG, Arthur A Six Months Tour Through the North of England 4 Vol
    (1770)

ABBREVIATIONS

Ch Soc   Chetham's Society
J R A S   Journal of the Royal Agricultural Society
Knutsford H A S   Knutsford Historic and Antiquarian Society
T H S L C   Transactions of the History Society of Lancashire and
    Cheshire
T L C A S   Transactions of the Lancashire and Cheshire Antiquarian
    Society
T R S L C   Transactions of the Record Society of Lancashire and
    Cheshire

BIBLIOGRAPHY

NEWSPAPERS & PERIODICALS

The Stockport Advertiser 1822-1980
The Stockport Advertiser Notes and Queries 1882-88
The Manchester Mercury 1788
Cheshire Notes and Queries 1886-1903
Lancashire Life February 1960
Manchester Guardian 1 August 1907

MANUSCRIPTS

Library of the University of Reading
The Diary of Peter Pownall. Acquisition no 146, November 1957, Farm
  (Records Collection

Stockport Central Library.
Mitchell, Frank. Notebook of a Country Farmer 1795-1806. S/43 621
The Burton Manuscripts. A History of Bramhall in the County of
    Manchester. 3 Vols S/62 E
Bramhall Township Books. Accounts of the Overseers of the Poor
    1821-1864. Bramhall Township Archives
Owen Manuscripts. Inscriptions on the Tombstones of St Mary's
    Church, Stockport. S/K22
Census Returns for Bramhall on microfilm. 1841 No 1316; 1852 No
    758; 1861 No 1336; 1871 Nos 303 & 4; 1881 No 1148.
The Registers of St Mary's Parish Church, Stockport 1584-1901,
    pp490-509
The Fairbank Plans 1739-1850. Copies relating to Bramhall at
    Stockport. Miscellaneous Maps 1022 (Originals in Sheffield
    City Library)

Cheshire County Record Office, Chester.
Census for Bramhall 1841 HO 108/1.
Consistory Court Papers showing farming of tithes EDC5(1662) No 81,
    (1683) No 115.
Court Rolls for Bramhall 1716-1732 DDA 1533/1
Examples of Davenport Lease, mentioning Peter Pownall 7 October 1797
    DDA 1384/199/4; Conveyance of Pepper Street Farm from Davenport
    to Pownall 1843 DDA 1384/205 A/16.
Examples of Leases showing marling, restrictions on potato growing,
    use of the mill etc. Box of Deeds of the Davenports of
    Bramhall 1500-1800 DDA/1533/1.
Examples of Poor Relief Accounts 1731-1837 P10/12; Settlement Papers
    1694-1839 P10/14; Removal Paper 1819 P10/13/27; Bastardy Papers
    1712-1835 P10/16; Bill for Maintenance P10/13/28; Overseers'
    Bill for Bramhall Workhouse 1819 P10 /13/21; Accounts for
    Bramhall Workhouse 1818 P10/13/15; Constables' Accounts 1834
    P10/14/8.

Land Tax Assessments for Bramhall 1713-16 DAR/A/69; Dar/A/70;
    DAR/C/28; DAR/D/58.
The Registers of Dean Row Unitarian Church, Wilmslow 2 Vols
    1749-1863 EUC1/1.
Tithe Map on Microfiche and Apportionment for Bramhall 1842
Wills and Inventories of many Bramhall residents until 1840 are
    available. WS & WI

MAPS

(In Stockport Central Library)
Burdett, P P County Map Vol 13 (1777)
Geographia Detailed Street Plan of Stockport (Modern)
Greenwood, C Map of the County Palatine of Chester (1819)
Ogilby, J The Continuation of the Road From York to West Chester
    (1675)
Ordnance Survey Buxton Sheet 27 (1805-73 Reprinted 1970)
Ordnance Survey Stockport Area 1:2500 (1872, 1896 & 1909) Sheet SJ
    98 (1934-49)
Plan of the Bramhall Estates belonging to the Freeholders Co. Ltd.
    (1877)
Plan of the Estates in the Township of Bramhall belonging to Mr John
    Hulme (1812)
Plan of the land in Bramhall leased by Mr John Carr from Thomas
    Brocklehurst Esq (1863)
Saxton, East Cheshire (1577)
Speed, John Cheshire (1610)
Stockport M B C Official Street Map of Hazel Grove and Bramhall
    4th Ed 1960
Tithe Commissioner's Map Bramhall (1842)

ILLUSTRATIONS

First page of the diary reproduced by kind permission of Reading
    University Library
Old St Mary's from Stockport Ancient and Modern, Vol 1, Henry Hegin-
    botham, 1882-92, p185
Sketches of Bramhall etc taken from old photographs collected by the
    group and copied by Stockport Library

INDEX

The index lists all the names and places that appear in the diary. Subject matter can be found in alphabetical order in the GLOSSARY.

The numbers refer to the pages in the original diary which are transcribed and printed above. The pages prefixed "Dp" (from page 65 onwards) have been transcribed and deposited, with an extended index including persons not mentioned in the diary, for consultation at Stockport Central Reference Library. These include pages 65-81, which contain the hours worked by casual labourers at harvest time (1786-1812); pp82-117, the names in the accounts, payments and receipts (1806-1808) and pp118-138, the accounts of the sale of farm produce (1790-1808).

INDEX

INDEX

Redfern, John 46, Dp 118, 121, 126, 127, 128, 129, 130, 131, 132,
     133, 134,
Richmond, Miss 34
Roads, Thomas 3, Dp 120
Robersons, [Robinson] Jonathan 51
Russel, Fanny 41

Salford 14
Shacroft, Thomas 3
Shaw, Joseph 12, 14, 15, Dp 118, 119, 123, 125, 126, 127, 128, 129,
     130, 132, 133, 134, 136, 137, 138
Shaw, Joshua 9, 20,29, 39
Shaw, Mrs 34
Skippen, Miss 22
Stand (school) 37, 38, 41, 45, 47, 55
Stockport 12, 17, 32, 38, 41, 44, 50, 51, 52, 53, 56, 57, 59, 63 Dp
     91, 129
Stockport Assembly 51, 59
Stockport Chapel 51
Stockport Church 57
Stockport Fair 3, 13, 19, 23, 25, 30, 34, 39, 52, 53, 58, 59, 60
Stockport Illuminations 63
Stockport Music Festival 57
Styal 6

Taylor, Henry 7
Taylor, Jane 51
Taylor, Mr 41, 46, Dp 121, 131

Walker, Lawrence 48
Walker, Mr 8
Wardle, Miss 18
Watson, Rev John 10, 12
Weston, Mr & Mrs 53, 59
Whitney, Mr 18
Williamson, Jereboam 14
Williamson, John 21
Wilmslow 33, 48, 57
Wilson [?School] 56
Wood, John 10
Wood, Joseph 9
Woodford (Witford) 6, 7, 14, 21, 22, 37
Woodford Races 27
Worthington, Mr 3, 6, 10, 50, 51, Dp 82, 83, 102, 103, 108, 113,
     118, 119, 121, 136
Worthington, Mr & Mrs 59
Worthington, Mr George 2, 34, 41
Worthington, Mr John 8,
Worthington, Mr, of Altrincham 50
Worthington, Mr Thomas 53
Wright, Miss 10
Wright, Mr 33